CONTENTS

Christmas Time

Ordinary Time during the Winter

Lent

Easter Time

✝

The Catholic Handbook for
Visiting the Sick and Homebound
2023
Year A

J. Philip Horrigan

LTP
LITURGY
TRAINING
PUBLICATIONS

Nihil Obstat
Deacon Daniel G. Welter, JD
Chancellor
Archdiocese of Chicago
April 7, 2022

Imprimatur
Most. Rev. Robert G. Casey
Vicar General
Archdiocese of Chicago
April 7, 2022

The *Nihil Obstat* and *Imprimatur* are declarations that the material is free from doctrinal or moral error, and thus is granted permission to publish in accordance with c. 827. No legal responsibility is assumed by the grant of this permission. No implication is contained herein that those who have granted the *Nihil Obstat* and *Imprimatur* agree with the content, opinions, or statements expressed.

Ordinary Time during the Summer and Fall

INTRODUCTION

Come to me, all you who labor and are burdened,
and I will give you rest. Take my yoke upon you and
learn from me, for I am meek and humble of heart;
and you will find rest for yourselves. For my yoke is
easy, and my burden light.

—Matthew 11:28–30

Suffering wears a thousand faces, and every face is Christ's. When we suffer sickness, loss, violence, or the harsher effects of aging in ourselves or in those we love, we cannot really understand the reasons, but we can choose the rock on which we will stand. We are members of the Body of Christ. Christ our Head is present in our suffering. In our dying we share his death. His voyage through death to the glory of the Resurrection becomes our journey. In him, we are held securely in the face of the anxiety, fear, anger, guilt, and grief that sickness, aging, or suffering can bring.

One of the deepest causes of suffering experienced by those whom sickness or aging confines to the narrow world of home, hospital, or geriatric facility is a sense of isolation. We may feel misunderstood, rejected, abandoned by the healthy world of which we were a part, even by those who love us, even by God. We feel that there is something wrong with us. We feel no longer useful. We cause other people discomfort and inconvenience. We may know how we "ought" to pray in times of suffering, but we can't seem to do it. We can't even go to church.

When we have suffered traumatic loss or violence, we may suffer a similar sense of loneliness. Our experience has set us apart. We may feel that no one can understand what we have endured. We find ourselves unable to take an interest in the world of everyday concerns about which others are busy. We may even find ourselves ill at ease with our ordinary companions in faith and worship. Even God may seem to have withdrawn to a safe distance. Our usual forms of prayer no longer seem to suffice. We have questions that are difficult to answer: Why me? Why has God allowed this to happen? We may be angry with God and ashamed of our anger. On the other hand, we may find ourselves more deeply in communion with the suffering Christ or with his bereaved and sorrowful Mother than before, yet separated from others by the intensity of our spiritual experience.

Ministers of care, both lay and the ordained, are sent to step across the chasm that isolates the sufferers, bringing them the comfort of personal presence and prayer. Ministries of care are as diverse as the parishes that sponsor them. Some parishes may have full-time lay pastoral associates or other employees who specialize in pastoral care. These laypeople may have been specially trained. They may have participated in pastoral care internships (Clinical Pastoral Education), or sought degrees in pastoral care or received diocesan or national certification. Parishes may also be fortunate enough to have volunteers who provide pastoral care to those in hospitals, hospices, nursing homes, prisons, police stations, crisis centers, and to those who are dying or have lost a loved one. These volunteers can provide music, proclaim Scripture, offer words of consolation and hope, or simply give the gift of silent presence.

The most familiar ministry of care is that of extraordinary minister of Holy Communion. The word *extraordinary* can be confusing. In this case, the Church uses it officially to distinguish between ordained bishops, priests, and deacons, who are the *ordinary* ministers of Holy Communion, and specially commissioned laypeople who fill the gaps, so to speak, when there are not enough ordinary ministers to give Holy Communion to everyone at Mass or to take Holy Communion to the sick and the homebound. The words *extraordinary* and *ordinary* as they are used here may seem odd because they recall a time when there were so many priests that there was no need for laypeople to take on this role.

This handbook is specially designed for the use of lay ministers of care, so it does not contain the rites for the Sacraments of Penance or the Anointing of the Sick, or the special prayers and blessings used by ordained bishops, priests, or deacons. All lay ministers who provide care to those who are sick, homebound, isolated, or suffering in some way will benefit from the contents of this book.

You, as a minister of care, have been called to be a sign and a bridge. Sent by the parish, you are the living witness that the community of faith and worship has not forgotten the absent sick, the invisible elderly, and the unseen sufferers. Praying with them as a representative of Christ living in the Church, you are a sign that God is and wants to be with them. You draw them back into awareness of their communion with the whole Body of Christ. They, and in many cases their caregivers, discover through you that they are not alone.

The Church has provided two official books containing a wealth of rites for those who visit, pray with, or bring Holy Communion to the sick, aging, dying, or others who are struggling with addiction, personal violence, or the loss of a child through miscarriage—especially those cut off from full participation in the liturgical life of their local Church or parish. These ritual books are called *Pastoral Care of the Sick: Rites of Anointing and Viaticum* and the *Book of Blessings. Pastoral Care of the Sick* contains rites specific to those who are sick and dying, providing orders of prayer for visits to the sick and for the Sacraments of Eucharist, Penance, and Anointing of the Sick. The *Book of Blessings* provides multiple orders of blessing for various needs and occasions. What you have in your hand, *The Catholic Handbook for Visiting the Sick and Homebound 2023* contains all of the rituals from *Pastoral Care of the Sick* and the *Book of Blessings* that can be used by laypeople when visiting the sick and the homebound. Everything you will need is right here! You will be able to use this book when you are sent to give Holy Communion to other parishioners or pray with those who are confined to their homes, to hospitals, or to geriatric centers; those who have suffered the traumatic loss of a child through miscarriage; those who suffer from addictions; and those who have been victims of violence. The most important resource you have as a minister, though, is your personal relationship with Christ, our healer and our Savior. You too are the face of Christ.

USING THIS BOOK

The Catholic Handbook for Visiting the Sick and Homebound 2023 will tell you what the Church asks of you, as her spokesperson, to say and do when you visit, pray with, or give Holy Communion to those who suffer. You need not worry about making up prayers—they are provided here for you! In fact, except where the rite itself calls for adaptation, you must use the prayers as they are written because they express the common faith of the Catholic Church to which we all committed ourselves in Baptism.

CONTENTS OF THIS BOOK

You, as a minister of care, will be called upon to offer those whom you visit an opportunity to benefit from the strengthening power of prayer by making use of one of the many rites and orders of prayer and blessing provided by the Church. This book contains everything you will need to give Holy Communion and lead further rites for praying with the sick and others who suffer for various reasons. The rites and prayers are divided into three sections:

- Orders for the Blessing of the Sick

- Pastoral Care of the Sick

- Section 3: Pastoral Care of the Dying

Each of these sections contains the official rites and orders of prayer as provided by the Church in both the *Book of Blessings* and *Pastoral Care of the Sick: Rites of Anointing and Viaticum.*

Blessings of and Visits to the Sick and Suffering

Visiting and Blessing the Sick.   You may be sent to visit the sick simply to pray with them. However, sometimes you may be prepared to give Holy Communion, but you discover that those you are visiting are unable to receive for some reason. At still other times, you may be visiting Catholic patients in an institution, but others who are not Catholic recognize you as a minister and ask you to pray with them. You need not turn away, feeling that you have nothing to offer. These are just a few of the situations when you could use these rites for visiting the sick and the suffering—either to prepare them to receive Holy Communion during a later visit or simply to enable them to draw strength and comfort from the healing presence of Christ.

Titles of These Rites.   Some clarification about the titles of the services contained in this book is needed to prevent confusion. The book titled *Pastoral Care of the Sick: Rites of Anointing and Viaticum* provides two rites for visiting the sick: "Visits to the Sick" and "Visits to a Sick Child." "Visits to the Sick" is used with adults. These two rites from *Pastoral Care of the Sick* are simple prayers for visiting the sick. The *Book of Blessings* also provides two rites. These two rites are "Order for the Blessing of Adults" and "Order for the Blessing of Children." Here the word "order" simply means "order of service." These two "orders" present an entire service of optional song, Scripture, prayer, and blessing.

The Rites.   The "Orders for the Blessing of the Sick" begin with a simple Sign of the Cross and invitation to pray followed by a reading of the Word of God whereas "Visits to the Sick" begins with the reading. "Visits to the Sick" continues with the Lord's Prayer and a choice of concluding prayers designed to address some of the different circumstances in which the sick might find themselves. Consider your options in relation to the situation of the person you are visiting. If you happen to be visiting someone who isn't Catholic, you may use this order of service, but remember to remind them tactfully that Catholics end the Lord's Prayer after "deliver us from evil." If not, be prepared for them to add the longer ending, "for thine is the kingdom, the power and the glory" before the "Amen." Above all, you do not want to cause distress to anyone.

In the "Orders for the Blessing of the Sick," the Word of God may be followed with an explanation of the reading, then a litany of intercession. The Church urges the minister to encourage the sick to participate in Christ's redemptive work by uniting their sufferings to his and by praying for the needs of the world. Prayer for others is an effective antidote to the self-preoccupation to which sickness and aging can tempt us. Intercessions provide an excellent way to meet this need. You may allow participants the opportunity to add petitions of their own, but beware of causing embarrassment by prolonging the silence if it becomes clear that they have nothing to say.

Both the rites for "Visits to the Sick" and "Orders for the Blessing of the Sick" end with prayers of blessing which may be said over the person who is ill. The "Orders for the Blessing of the Sick" provides two prayers of blessing. The first option is for more than one person, whereas the second option is for a single individual. The rite stipulates that the minister is to make the Sign of the Cross on the forehead of the sick while saying the prayer. The gesture may be unexpected or unfamiliar, especially coming from a lay minister, so it is wise to let people know what you are preparing to do. The Sign of the Cross may be followed by a prayer for the protection of the Blessed Virgin Mary. The rite suggests singing a familiar Marian song. If music is unavailable, only sing if those you are visiting are able to participate.

"Orders for the Blessing of the Sick" and "Visits to the Sick" end with a concluding prayer. In both rites, the "lay minister invokes the Lord's blessing on the sick and all present by signing himself or herself with the Sign of the Cross."

"Visits to the Sick" includes two prayers of blessing, one for a sick person and one for the elderly. Please note that the lay minister does not make the same gesture as given in "Orders for the Blessing of the Sick." Simply say the prayer.

The "Order for the Blessing of Children" and "Visits to a Sick Child" follow the same pattern as those used for adults, but they use simpler language. You will have to decide which rite or order of blessing is appropriate to use with older children. A word of caution: Before you make the Sign of the Cross on the child's head during the blessing, it would be wise to alert parents or caregivers to see if they have any objections. It is also wise to explain this to the child. Remember that very sick children may have experienced unpleasant medical procedures and may fear the unexplained touch of an unfamiliar adult.

Visiting and Blessing Those Who Suffer.   *The Catholic Handbook for Visiting the Sick and Homebound 2023* includes three additional services for blessing those who suffer and may not be able to participate in Sunday Eucharist:

- Blessing a Person Suffering from Addiction or from Substance Abuse

- Blessing a Victim of Crime or Oppression

- Blessing Parents after a Miscarriage

You may meet people in need of one of these special blessings. You may meet them in a health care setting. For example, a patient may have been hospitalized as a result of addictive behavior or alcohol and drug abuse. Sometimes you may meet a patient who has suffered personal violence, such as domestic abuse, rape, a drive-by shooting, injuries sustained in an accident caused by a drunk driver or at the hands of those engaged in criminal activities such as robbery, or a person afflicted with posttraumatic stress disorder. You may also find that a woman has suffered a miscarriage, and she and the father are grieving together. You may also find people among the families of those you are visiting who ask you to pray with them or give them Holy Communion at home or in an institutional environment. An elderly person might indicate a child or grandchild who is suffering one of these needs and ask you to pray with them. You may be among those assigned to special ministries of care in settings such as support groups.

Be aware that the reason for the need may be recent or long standing. Sometimes, someone who is coping with illness, confinement in a geriatric facility, or other situation which has brought you to them will want to discuss something that happened long ago and continues to haunt them. Periods of inactivity brought on by sickness or aging give us plenty of time to think and may spur us to make peace with the past in a new way. These orders of blessing offer that opportunity.

Whenever you meet someone in one of these situations, you may use the appropriate order of blessing from the pages that follow. All of them follow the same pattern: an introductory rite (Sign of the Cross, simple greeting, optional introduction), reading and response, including the opportunity to comment on the reading, intercessions, the Lord's Prayer, a prayer of blessing directed to the particular needs of participants, and a concluding rite (general blessing). The Church encourages adaptation, provided the order of service is followed and the major elements included. For example, you might want to personalize the opening introduction, following the general pattern of the one provided here. Here is one example of a personalized introduction to the "Order for Blessing a Victim of Crime or Oppression." Imagine that you are praying with and for a young woman who is a victim of date rape. You might say something like this:

God has always shown care and compassion for people who have suffered acts of violence, like the one that has brought you here. We commend you, [**N.**: *use the woman's name*], to God, who binds up all our wounds, heals us from the pain of betrayal, and restores us to our rightful dignity as a child of God.

The introduction now refers to the victim's own experience, uses her name, and avoids language that could summon up frightening images of being held by a male person.

You will want to choose those intercessions that are most appropriate. You may invite participants to add their own, and you may also do so. Turning one's own suffering into prayer for others is both a way of uniting oneself with the redemptive suffering of Christ and a means of turning one's attention outward. If you are accustomed to using the "Orders for the Blessing of the Sick," please note that there are some differences between them and these orders of blessing for those otherwise in distress. In particular, these latter orders call for the Lord's Prayer, which often provides the comfort of a familiar prayer; and they do not call for the minister to touch the person while saying the prayer of blessing for them. This can be an important courtesy when using this order for blessing with those who have suffered personal violence and shy away from being touched by strangers, even in prayers of blessing.

Like the "Orders for the Blessing of the Sick," these orders also provide a shorter form: a short invitation to prayer, a short reading, and a prayer of blessing. These short forms are particularly useful when ministering to those who have very recently experienced a crisis in addiction, an incident of violence, or a miscarriage, and are too distressed to concentrate on a longer ritual. They are also helpful when you are visiting the person for some other reason and find a need to help them deal with one of these issues.

One of the hidden benefits of the Church's rites of prayer is that they teach us to think in harmony with the Church. If you have never experienced the particular need for which you are blessing someone, your good intentions may sometimes stumble in trying to find the right words of comfort. It is easy to offend without meaning to by offering what sound like platitudes to those who are in the immediate throes of suffering. It is also easy to give impressions of God that hurt rather than help them. The texts of these rites will assist you to reflect on how to focus your comments. They are also impersonal enough that they offer room for participants in the rites to take them as words from God to be pondered and applied to their own experience rather than as personal remarks about their own faith response to what they have suffered. Ministers must be particularly careful not to suggest when they speak spontaneously that the sufferer is being punished for a lack of faith or for slack religious practice or for some particular sin. Remember that anger with God, fear of God, a sense of alienation from God, and particularly a sense of despair often lurk at the edges of suffering. You want to encourage instead turning to God in trust and in hope. Even there, though, please be careful to allow room for those who want to turn to God in a positive way but are not yet emotionally ready to do so. God's love is profoundly patient.

Holy Communion

This book provides two rites for lay ministers to give Holy Communion to the sick: "Communion in Ordinary Circumstances" and "Communion in a Hospital or Institution."

Communion in Ordinary Circumstances. The first form, called "Communion in Ordinary Circumstances," is especially useful if you are taking Holy Communion to the sick or aging in their homes. It assumes two things: First, that you have enough time to lead the full rite of Holy Communion, including a short Liturgy of the Word; second, that those you visit are well enough to participate in a full service. The Church urges us always to consider the needs of the sick or aging. If they are very weak or tire quickly, it's better to shorten or omit elements like the explanation after the reading or the Universal Prayer or Prayer of the Faithful, or simply to use the shorter form called "Communion in a Hospital or Institution" even in a home setting.

Communion in a Hospital or Institution.   This second form, "Communion in a Hospital or Institution," provides a minimal format mainly intended for use when you are visiting many patients individually in an institutional setting. The Church expresses a strong preference for avoiding this abbreviated format even in an institution. Instead, it is suggested that, if possible, you gather several residents together in one or more areas and celebrate the full rite of "Communion in Ordinary Circumstances." If that is not possible, the Church recommends that you add elements from the fuller rite, such as the reading of the Word, unless participants are too weak. On the other hand, in the case of extremely sick people, you may shorten "Communion in a Hospital or Institution" by omitting as much of the rite as necessary. Try to include at least a greeting, the Lord's Prayer, the customary responses that precede Holy Communion itself, and the closing prayer. Please note that the "customary responses" have now been reworded. See the section on page 18 on using the new translation from the third edition of *The Roman Missal* for those prayers taken from the Order of Mass for use in the Rites of Communion.

Pastoral Care of the Dying

Viaticum, Holy Communion for the Dying.   Any of the seriously ill, but especially hospice patients, may move more quickly than expected toward death. A person who faces death within days should receive Holy Communion under the form of Viaticum. *Viaticum* means something like "travel with you," but it is often translated as "food for the journey." Although the Sacrament of Anointing of the Sick strengthens us in the face of sickness, Eucharist as Viaticum is the sacrament that, together with Penance, prepares a person for the final journey through death to everlasting life in Christ. Catholics are obligated to receive Viaticum if possible. The Sacrament of Anointing of the Sick may be given after Penance but before Viaticum. If the person is unable to swallow, they may receive the

Sacrament of Anointing from a priest instead of Viaticum; however, the Church teaches that Viaticum is the essential sacrament when we are in the face of death. The time for using the special comforting and strengthening prayers of the Rite of Viaticum to administer Holy Communion is while the person is still conscious and able to swallow. Once death has become imminent, dying persons may receive Viaticum every day for as long as they are able. An extraordinary minister of Holy Communion may and should give Viaticum to the dying. If the dying person has not received sacramental absolution, please make sure the person has the opportunity for both the Sacrament of Penance and, if desired, Anointing of the Sick.

Commendation for the Dying and Prayers for the Dead. While the sacraments, especially Viaticum, unite the dying with Christ in his passage from this life to the next, we also gather with the dying and those around them to sustain this union through the prayer and faith of the Church.

"Commendation for the Dying" does not follow a fixed pattern. You may select any texts from the prayers, litanies, aspirations, psalms, and readings, or you may use other familiar prayers, such as the Rosary. If you have had the opportunity to talk with the dying person and loved ones or others present, choose texts you think will sustain and strengthen them according to their spiritual needs and other circumstances. Pray the texts slowly and quietly, allowing ample opportunities for silence. You may repeat them as often as needed, especially prayers that have special meaning for those present. Even those who are unconscious and dying can sometimes hear more than we realize. If the dying cannot hear, loved ones present will find comfort in the prayers.

If you minister in an institutional setting, you may find that those who are not Catholic will ask you to pray with and for them. You may use these texts with and for any who are in need of the consolation of prayer. The texts drawn from the Bible are especially likely to bring comfort.

Once death has occurred, you will find both prayers for the dead and prayers for family and friends on page 133, "Prayers for the Dead."

Ritual Preparation. All of the rites are simple to follow. Look them over before making your visits in order to familiarize yourself with the order of prayer. Directions are included and parts are clearly marked so that you can easily lead the assembly in prayer.

The Gospel for Sundays and Holydays of Obligation

Following the rites is the Gospel for Sundays and Holydays of Obligation for Year A. The Church has a three-year cycle of readings. In 2023, the readings will be from Year A. It is recommended to use the Sunday Gospel during the rites for Holy Communion as one important way of uniting the communicants in spirit with the parish from which sickness or age has separated them.

In this book, the Gospel is clearly labeled by date and the title of particular observances so that you can easily find the appropriate reading. For example, if you make your visit during the Second Week of Lent, you will use the Gospel for the Second Sunday of Lent. In 2023, this Sunday of Lent is March 5. Simply look for the date and the title of the celebration and you will know which Gospel to use. For some observances, such as Palm Sunday, the Lectionary provides a longer and shorter form of the Gospel. For simplicity, only the shorter form is included in this resource.

If you are visiting on a Holyday of Obligation, use the Gospel prescribed for these days. You can also locate the Gospel for Holydays of Obligation by date and title. In the dioceses of the United States of America, the Holydays of Obligation occurring in the 2023 liturgical year are:

- Solemnity of the Immaculate Conception of the Blessed Virgin Mary (December 8, 2022)

- Solemnity of the Nativity of the Lord (December 25, 2022)

- Solemnity of Mary, the Holy Mother of God (January 1, 2023)

- Solemnity of the Ascension of the Lord (May 18 or 21, 2023)

- Solemnity of the Assumption of the Blessed Virgin Mary (August 15, 2023)

- Solemnity of All Saints (November 1, 2023)

If you are visiting very young sick children, you might want to obtain a copy of the appropriate reading from the *Lectionary for Masses with Children* from your parish. Another option is to read the Gospel passages recommended in "Visits to a Sick Child."

If you are praying with those who are struggling with addictions, the aftermath of violence, or with parents who have suffered the loss of a child through miscarriage, you will usually find the readings recommended in the orders of blessing more appropriate to their circumstances than the

Gospel for the Sunday. However, if appropriate, feel free to use the Gospel for Sundays and Holydays of Obligation. To discern which readings to use, it is best to look over the order of service before the visit occurs.

Explanation of the Readings

You will notice that the rites offer an opportunity for the minister of care to give a brief explanation of the reading with special reference to the experience of those with whom you are praying and, where appropriate, of their caregivers. If you are using the Sunday or Holyday reading, you might want to base your explanation of the reading on the parish Sunday Homily in order to deepen the sense of connection you are trying to encourage. If you feel uncomfortable about speaking, you will find a brief explanation of the reading after the Gospel for each Sunday and Holyday. If you choose to read it from the book, it would be a good idea to ponder it and make it your own so that the words come from your heart and not merely from the page. The Word of God itself creates a bond between reader and hearers, breaking down the sense of isolation that afflicts sufferers. Explanatory words that are spoken, or even read, with sincerity and personal conviction will support this pastoral relationship more effectively than words read mechanically.

Patron Saints

Finally, there is a list of saints who the Church has identified as particular intercessors, companions, and guides for those suffering various kinds of afflictions, whether physical or emotional. If you feel that those with whom you pray would welcome the company and support of a saint, you might want to include the saint's name in the intercessions and suggest that those you are visiting continue to ask for the saint's help. An example of an intercession is:

> For all those who suffer from throat cancer, especially **N.** (*insert the name of the person or persons present*), that through the intercession of Saint Blaise, they may find comfort and strength, we pray to the Lord.

This book does not provide any information about the saints listed, but there are many books and websites where you can find their stories. Such resources are *Companion to the Calendar, Second Edition* (Liturgy Training Publications) and *Butler's Lives of the Saints* (published by The Liturgical Press).

BEYOND THE BOOK

The official rites offer appropriate prayers and clear directions, but they don't tell you everything you need to know in order to lead the rituals effectively. Here are some practical hints that may help.

Getting from the Parish Church to Your Pastoral Assignment

Scheduling a Visit. Some parishes assign ministers to visit particular people but encourage them to make their own arrangements regarding the day and time. Both those in need of your ministry and their families or caregivers, at home or in institutional facilities, appreciate being able to negotiate appropriate times for a pastoral visit or Holy Communion. It gives them an opportunity to make sure that they and those they would like to have present can be there. For example, if you're visiting the sick, you don't want to drop in when patients are absent from their rooms for tests or treatments.

If you are asked to take Holy Communion to the sick and the home-bound at times other than during Sunday Mass, please make sure your training includes information about where to find the tabernacle key and how to approach the tabernacle reverently, open it, and transfer the hosts you will need from the ciborium in which they are kept to the container you will use to carry the Blessed Sacrament to the sick (see below). It is particularly important to arrange with the parish coordinator a convenient time for you to obtain the tabernacle key, because it is not permitted to keep the Eucharist at home or carry it all day as you go about your ordinary business before visiting communicants.

Ordinarily, when taking the Blessed Sacrament from the tabernacle, you would pray briefly before the tabernacle, wash your fingers in a small vessel of water that is usually kept beside the tabernacle for that purpose, wipe them on a finger towel also usually kept there, and genuflect after opening the tabernacle. If your parish does not provide either the small vessel or finger towel, wash your hands in the sacristy or otherwise clean your fingers as best you are able over the sacrarium (a sink flowing directly into the ground for water from purifications, from the first washings of the altar cloths, or the water containing the completely dissolved conse-crated hosts which cannot be properly consumed).

If you have unused hosts left over at the end of your rounds, you must bring them back to the parish church and replace them in the tabernacle.

After closing the tabernacle, you again wash your fingers. You may also cleanse the empty pyx (a dignified vessel, often round, used to carry the consecrated host) in the sacrarium if it appears to contain crumbs. Fill it with water, drink the water, and dry the pyx carefully on a finger towel, if available.

If you wish to avoid having hosts that must be returned, you can give the last few communicants more than one host so that all the hosts are consumed or consume them yourself as part of the Communion Rite during your last visit, provided all the usual requirements for Holy Communion are met. However, you may not simply consume them yourself after your last visit because Holy Communion is always received in the context of public prayer rather than simply as a matter of convenience by the minister alone. Similarly, you may not take the remaining hosts home to return later to the church because the Eucharist must be kept in a tabernacle or other designated locked place of reservation in a church.

Bringing What You Need.   Make a checklist of what you want to have with you before you leave home. You'll find some suggestions below. Don't forget this book! It does happen. If it does, don't panic, and don't fail to keep your appointment. As a precaution, make every effort to memorize the outline of the rites you expect to use or keep a copy of a simple outline in your pocket, wallet, or purse. In this case, do make up your own prayer, but keep it very short and simple. Borrow a Bible or summarize the Gospel in your own words. God works through all our weaknesses and mistakes.

Carrying the Blessed Sacrament.   The Blessed Sacrament is carried in the pyx or in another dignified vessel reserved exclusively for that purpose. Your parish will probably supply you with what you need. Some pyxes can be worn or carried in a pouch on a cord around the neck. When you are carrying the Blessed Sacrament, remember and attend reverently to Christ, choosing your activities appropriately, without becoming artificially silent or stilted in your conversation, especially with those who are not aware of what you are carrying or of its significance. On the one hand, avoid distractions such as loud music, "talk" programs or other television shows, movies or DVDs/tapes, or other things that would disturb prayer while you are en route. On the other hand, while avoiding such distractions, be careful not to be rude to people who greet you or speak to you in passing as you walk to your destination. Christ is not offended by the company and conversation of human beings! You should make your Communion visit immediately upon leaving the Church.

Music Preparation.   Sometimes it might be possible to incorporate music into your visits. Music most certainly can be included in the rites and orders of blessing. Singing familiar melodies and texts can be extremely comforting and healing to those who are suffering. Hospitals, nursing homes, and other facilities might have a piano or you might bring a guitar. A capella singing can be just as effective. Be sure to select music in which either the refrain is simple or the melodies are familiar. Choose texts that give a message of the hope we have in Christ. Here are some suggestions: "Blest Are They" (Haas), "Jesus, Heal Us" (Haas), "Healer of Our Every Ill" (Haugen), "Lord of All Hopefulness" (traditional), "I Heard the Voice of Jesus Say" (traditional), "Remember Your Love" (Balhoff), "Shepherd Me, O God" (Haugen), and "You Are Mine" (Haas).

Preparing an Environment for Prayer: Encountering Christ in Persons

Church ministry is always personal. It is important that you spend a few minutes at the beginning of your visit to get to know those present and give them a chance to feel comfortable with you. Your parish may be able to supply you with helpful information in advance.

When you arrive, put those present at ease by engaging in a few moments of personal conversation. Tell them your name and remind them that the parish has sent you. Ask how they are and listen attentively to their answers. If you are visiting the sick, show your interest and concern, but remember that you are not there to offer medical advice or to pass judgment on medical matters, even if you yourself are a professional medical caregiver. If you can, address those you are visiting by name, but be aware that not everyone likes to be addressed by a first name without permission. Sickness, debilitating aging, and other forms of public suffering often rob people of their sense of personal dignity, so treating people with respect is an important dimension of your ministry. Whatever their condition, you and they are both collaborators in Christ's work. Ministry is a two-way street: those whom you visit are serving you by their witness to Christ's suffering as much as you are serving them by offering them Christ's loving comfort. Take note of any special needs you see: is the sufferer low on energy, in pain, limited in motion, hard of hearing, angry, sad, or seemingly depressed? You will want to tailor the length, content, and style of the celebration accordingly.

Preparing Yourself to Lead Prayer

The world of the suffering, especially those confined to home or, even more so, to a hospital or geriatric facility may not feel much like a place of prayer. The most important element in creating an environment for prayer is you. The minister who prays while leading others in prayer is the most powerful invitation one can offer to those who need to be called from all the preoccupations of suffering into deeper awareness of the mystery of God present and acting in our midst.

Here are some steps you can take to develop this important skill:

- Devote time to praying, reading, and meditating on the texts of the prayers and readings provided in this book. You will best pray them in public if you have already prayed them many times in private.

- Familiarize yourself thoroughly with the structure and flow of the rites so that you can concentrate on the people rather than the book. You need not memorize prayers or readings. Simply know what comes next and where to find it.

- Before you go into the building or room, pray briefly, asking Christ to work through you; after the visit, pause to give thanks.

- Reflect on your experience after you return home. Were there moments during the celebration when you felt uncertain or distracted? Why? What could you do next time to make yourself more at ease so that you can pray more attentively without losing contact with those you are leading in prayer? Sharing experience with other ministers of care or parish staff can be a useful way to continue and deepen everyone's ministry formation.

Preparing the Room for Prayer

You can also take some simple steps to establish an atmosphere that encourages prayer when circumstances allow. A small standing crucifix, cross, or icon heightens consciousness of Christ. Appropriate lighting can help, where possible. In an institutional setting, for example, a lamp or sunlight creates a more calming environment than do fluorescent lights. If you are taking Holy Communion to someone, take a small white cloth and a candle with you to prepare a place to put the pyx containing the Blessed Sacrament as a focus for the celebration as you lead the other prayers. (Be sure you have something with which to light the candle!) A corporal (traditionally a square, white, linen cloth upon which is placed sacred vessels holding the Blessed Sacrament) is not required, but if it is used, it is traditionally placed on top of another white cloth rather than on a bare surface. Caregivers familiar with the rite may have prepared a place in advance, but many will not.

Be aware of the restrictions you may face in a health care or geriatric facility. The rites for Holy Communion recommend that the minister be accompanied by a candle-bearer and place a candle on the table where the Blessed Sacrament will stand during the celebration, as described above. However, safety regulations usually forbid the use of open flames in institutions. Oxygen and other substances that might be in use are highly flammable. Moreover, you may not be able to find any appropriate surface other than a bedside table or night stand that will have to be cleared before you can set up a place for the Blessed Sacrament. Be prepared to make whatever practical adjustments the circumstances require. If you have never visited a particular hospital unit or nursing home, see if you can find another minister who has and find out what to expect.

Preparing Participants for Prayer

After a few moments of conversation, find a graceful way to end the social part of the visit without seeming uninterested or abrupt. Then give the participants a simple, brief overview of the rite you will be using so they will know what to expect, unless you know they are already familiar with the rite. Surprises tend to disrupt prayer! It's especially important to decide in advance who will do the reading. The directions say that the reading may be done "by one of those present or by the minister." If you don't know the participants, the best solution might be to ask for a volunteer (and allow the volunteer a few moments to prepare), but remember that not everyone is willing or able to read in public with short notice, especially in times of distress. Finally, mark the beginning of prayer clearly by inviting silent attentiveness, making the Sign of the Cross and moving into the service itself.

Recognizing the Recipient

You are ministering not only to those to whom the ritual is addressed but also to those around them, whether loved ones or caregivers. Be sure to include them by looking at them and speaking to them, as well as to the person who is your focus. When you are saying prayers of blessing over the sufferer, your attention is on that person alone, but all present are invited to join in the "Amen" that affirms and concludes the prayer. Practice with another minister until you can say prayers in such a way that others know when and how to respond without having a book in front of them.

Who May Receive Holy Communion?

Catholic shut-ins, caregivers, or others who assemble with them may receive Holy Communion provided the usual conditions have been met. You can offer that invitation before you begin the rite for Holy Communion, being careful not to embarrass or offend those who are not eligible to receive. "The elderly, the infirm and those who care for them can receive the Holy Eucharist even if they have eaten something within the preceding hour" (*Code of Canon Law,* 919 §2).

Special Circumstances

Unfortunately, neither sickness nor the deterioration sometimes brought on by aging is neat or predictable. The physical, psychological, and spiritual condition of those you visit may have changed since the arrangements for your visit were made. You may need to make unprepared changes in the rite or blessing you are using to meet the current need.

Special Circumstances for Extraordinary Ministers of Holy Communion

If you are taking Holy Communion to the sick or elderly, sometimes those you are visiting will express reluctance to receive. They may or may not want to tell you why. They might be embarrassed to say that they are too nauseated; they might feel alienated from God; they might need sacramental absolution but don't want to say so. You are obviously a person of generosity and compassion, or you wouldn't have volunteered to be an extraordinary minister of Holy Communion. However, a Holy Communion visit is not ordinarily the best time to identify and try to resolve serious personal or spiritual problems. Be aware of your status and of the vulnerability of the suffering: You represent the Church, and you have more power than you may realize to make others feel guilty by showing that you disapprove of their decision not to receive Holy Communion or by giving the impression that they have wasted your time. Remember that they are not rejecting you as a person. Rather, they are struggling with something deeper. Offer to pray with them, using the rites provided for visiting or blessing the sick. Invite them to enter more deeply into communion with the suffering and risen Christ who loves them. Let them know what pastoral resources are available to them: offer to return or to send another minister at a more convenient time; provide the parish phone number; offer to let the pastoral staff know that they would like a priest to visit, without forcing them to reply. If the parish distributes a bulletin during the weekend Masses, bring one along to leave with the person you are visiting.

Sometimes you may find that those you are visiting are unable to swallow easily. Consult medical caregivers. If they give permission, you may break the host into the smallest of pieces, place a piece on the person's tongue to dissolve, and follow with a glass of water to make swallowing possible. Be careful with crumbs when you break the host. The best thing to do is to break the host carefully over the pyx so that crumbs will fall into the pyx. If any crumbs fall on the cloth or table on which the pyx has been placed, moisten your finger, pick up all the crumbs very carefully, and consume them reverently.

You may even find that someone cannot ingest the host at all. In such cases, the person may receive the Blood of Christ, but that requires specialized vessels and procedures. Report the circumstances to your pastor, parish coordinator, or to the facility chaplain's office if the person is in a health care or geriatric facility. They will be able to give Holy Communion appropriately. In the meantime, use one of the rites for visiting or blessing the sick to give them the support of your presence and prayer.

Be aware that the hospitalized may not be permitted to take anything by mouth for a period of time prior to certain tests or treatments. Even a small piece of the host received at such times may cause medical personnel to cancel the planned procedure. If you see a sign that says "Nothing by mouth" or "NPO," initials for the Latin phrase *nil per os,* meaning the same thing, ask a member of the medical staff if you may administer Holy Communion, but expect a "no." In this case, too, you should still pray with the sick or aging, using one of the rites for visiting or blessing the sick. Remember that you still offer them the comfort of Christ's presence in his Word and through your own presence and that of the parish you represent.

Don't be alarmed by moments of silence. Sometimes ministers think they need to fill silences with conversation or action. There is nothing wrong with sitting in silence with another. In fact, these can be quite healing moments. God is present in the silence.

You should also be cognizant of those who are either not able to speak, have difficulty speaking, or speak rather slowly. Be patient and allow them to respond as they are able.

It is important that the extraordinary minister of Holy Communion keeps in mind the sacramental rites which are an essential part of the Church's ministry to the sick and dying and which can be administered only by an ordained bishop or priest—the Sacraments of Reconciliation and the Anointing of the Sick. As appropriate, it is part of your ministry to bring these to the attention of the sick and those confined to their homes, and if needed, to help them contact a priest.

Using the New Translation of Mass Responses in Prayer

The changes made to *The Roman Missal* in 2011 still present some challenges when visiting the ill and homebound. Some of the texts in the rites for the sick and dying were borrowed from the Mass, so they must also be used in the new translation. In collaboration with the United States Conference of Catholic Bishops (USCCB) and the International Commission on English in the Liturgy Corporation (ICEL) this edition of *The Catholic Handbook for Visiting the Sick and Homebound* has been updated with the proper texts.

This change in translation poses two pastoral challenges for ministers of care. The first is to familiarize yourself with the new texts so that you can use them comfortably without awkward pauses or repetitions. Your own sense of ease allows participants to relax and concentrate on receiving Christ prayerfully rather than paying attention to you. It has been suggested that the previous translation of the Mass might be used with those confused by illness, trauma, or age, but that does not seem necessary in celebrations of Communion for such recipients. The changes in the ministers' texts are minimal. The previous texts are probably not particularly familiar to most people because they have never actually had to say them personally. They are unlikely to notice that the texts have a slightly different wording now, as long as you give them the proper cue word for their responses. For example, after you have said, "Behold the Lamb of God, / behold him who takes away the sins of the world. / Blessed are those called to the supper of the Lamb," you can ease participants into the correct response by looking at them, nodding your head, and starting them out on "Lord, I am not worthy . . . " That technique can be useful even with familiar texts that people are not accustomed to reciting solo!

The second challenge requires pastoral sensitivity and discernment. It will take some time for the new translation to become a habit for worshippers. You will sometimes be taking Communion to people who have not been able to attend Mass since the new translations were introduced and so are unfamiliar with them. You will be visiting others who are traumatized by strange surroundings, illness, age, and distress. Under those circumstances, the old texts will come much more easily to mind for many. Please remember that your primary task is pastoral care, not catechesis. If participants make the old responses and you try to correct them, you will introduce a note of uncertainty and discomfort that may keep them from the communion with Christ in prayer that they so badly need. In some cases, you might provide them with participation aids that contain the appropriate responses. However, they may or may not find such aids useful. Not everyone reads easily. Some will have lost track of their glasses. Others may be unable to hold the aids steady enough to read them. The light may be too poor or the text too small for some. You will need to assess the circumstances and make an on-the-spot decision about whether or not to give them whatever aids you may have brought. Fostering prayer is your primary goal. While you yourself must use the correct texts, the correctness of participants' responses is secondary.

Service to the People of God

Among these nuts and bolts of the ministry of care, never lose sight of your purpose. You have been commissioned in the name of Christ and his Church to serve as a bridge builder across the isolation that separates the sick and suffering from the parish community of faith and worship. Your deepest task is to carry the Good News of the Gospel to those who stand in need of its healing power. However, the most important tool is one that only Christ can provide for you. The more deeply you yourself enter into the heart of the Gospel message, the more clearly you will see that sick and healthy, young and old, grieving and rejoicing, struggling and at peace, are all one Body. In that Body, we are all servants of the Good News we proclaim, building one another up in faith and love until that day when, by God's gracious gift, we will all dwell together in the Lord's own house for ever and ever.

Genevieve Glen, osb

About the Authors

Genevieve Glen, OSB, is a Benedictine nun of the contemplative Abbey of St. Walburga in Virginia Dale, Colorado. She holds master's degrees in systematic theology from Saint John's University, Collegeville, Minnesota, and in spirituality from the Catholic University of America in Washington DC, where she also did extensive doctoral studies in liturgy. She has lectured and written extensively on the Church's rites for the sick and dying. She is co-author of the *Handbook for Ministers of Care, third edition* (upcoming from Liturgy Training Publications) and contributing editor of *Recovering the Riches of Anointing: A Study of the Sacrament of the Sick* (Liturgical Press).

Rev. J. Philip Horrigan is a presbyter of the Archdiocese of Kingston, Ontario. He has a graduate degree in theology (MTH, 1994– 95) from the Institute for Spirituality and Worship at the Jesuit School of Theology at Berkeley, CA. In June 1997 he received his doctorate of ministry (DMIN, liturgical studies) at Catholic Theological Union in Chicago, and was appointed the director of the newly formed Department for Art and Architecture in the Office for Divine Worship, Archdiocese of Chicago, a position he held for twelve and a half years. In this capacity he acted as a liturgical consultant/resource person for all the new church building and renovation projects for the Archdiocese, and chaired the Diocesan Commission on Church Art and Architecture. He is an adjunct faculty in the Word and Worship department at Catholic Theological Union, Chicago. Since 2009 he has developed his ministry as a liturgical design consultant and maintains a number of consulting projects in Canada and the United States, both with Roman Catholic and Lutheran congregations. He is a frequent presenter at conferences and workshops on various topics related to the building and renovation of worship spaces, as well as issues on the liturgical environment, the history and components of liturgical design, sacramental theology, the spiritual and ecclesial dimensions of liturgical ministries, and the pastoral implications of liturgicalrituals, documents, and praxis. He has written a number of articles for liturgical publications and his particular interest is understanding and exploring the relationship between ritual space and ritual event.

THE RITES

Orders for the Blessing of the Sick

INTRODUCTION

376   The blessing of the sick by the ministers of the Church is a very ancient custom, having its origins in the practice of Christ himself and his apostles. When ministers visit those who are sick, they are to respect the provisions of *Pastoral Care of the Sick: Rites of Anointing and Viaticum,* nos. 42–56, but the primary concern of every minister should be to show the sick how much Christ and his Church are concerned for them.

377   The text of *Pastoral Care of the Sick* indicates many occasions for blessing the sick and provides the blessing for formularics.[13]

378   The present order may be used by a priest or deacon. It may also be used by a layperson, who follows the rites and prayers designated for a lay minister. While maintaining the structure and chief elements of the rite, the minister should adapt the celebration to the circumstances of the place and the people involved.

379   When just one sick person is to be blessed, a priest or deacon may use the short formulary given in no. 406.

---

13.   See Roman Ritual, Pastoral Care of the Sick: Rites of Anointing and Viaticum, no. 54.

ORDER OF BLESSING

A. ORDER FOR THE BLESSING OF ADULTS
INTRODUCTORY RITES

380   When the community has gathered, the minister says:

In the name of the Father, and of the Son, and of the
Holy Spirit.

All make the sign of the cross and reply:

Amen.

382   A lay minister greets those present in the following words.

Brothers and sisters, let us bless the Lord, who went about doing
good and healing the sick. Blessed be God now and for ever.

R. *Blessed be God now and for ever.*

Or:

R. *Amen.*

*383   In the following or similar words, the minister prepares the sick
and all present for the blessing.*

The Lord Jesus, who went about doing good works and
healing sickness and infirmity of every kind, commanded his
disciples to care for the sick, to pray for them, and to lay hands
on them. In this celebration we shall entrust our sick brothers
and sisters to the care of the Lord, asking that he will enable
them to bear their pain and suffering in the knowledge that,
if they accept their share in the pain of his own passion, they
will also share in its power to give comfort and strength.

Reading of the Word of God

384   A reader, another person present, or the minister reads a text of sacred Scripture, taken preferably from the texts given in Pastoral Care of the Sick *and the* Lectionary for Mass.[14] *The readings chosen should be those that best apply to the physical and spiritual condition of those who are sick.*

**Brothers and sisters, listen to the words of
the second letter of Paul to the Corinthians:**   1:3–7

The God of all consolation.

Blessed be the God and Father of our Lord Jesus Christ, the Father of compassion and God of all encouragement, who encourages us in our every affliction, so that we may be able to encourage those who are in any affliction with the encouragement with which we ourselves are encouraged by God. For as Christ's sufferings overflow to us, so through Christ does our encouragement also overflow. If we are afflicted, it is for your encouragement and salvation; if we are encouraged, it is for your encouragement, which enables you to endure the same sufferings that we suffer. Our hope for you is firm, for we know that as you share in the sufferings, you also share in the encouragement.

385   Or:

**Brothers and sisters, listen to the words of
the holy gospel according to Matthew:**   11:28–30

Come to me and I will refresh you.

Jesus said to the crowds: "Come to me, all you who labor and are burdened, and I will give you rest. Take my yoke upon you and learn from me, for I am meek and humble of heart;

---

14.   See ibid, no. 297; Lectionary for Mass (2nd ed., 1981), nos. 790–795, 796–800 (Ritual Masses: V. Pastoral Care of the Sick and the Dying, 1. Anointing of the Sick and 2. Viaticum), and nos. 933–937 (Masses for Various Needs and Occasions, III. For Various Public Needs, 24. For the Sick).

and you will find rest for yourselves. For my yoke is easy, and my burden light."

386   *Or:*

**Brothers and sisters, listen to the words of
the holy gospel according to Mark:**   6:53–56
They laid the sick in the marketplace.

After making the crossing, Jesus and his disciples came to land at Gennesaret and tied up there. As they were leaving the boat, people immediately recognized him. They scurried about the surrounding country and began to bring in the sick on mats to wherever they heard he was. Whatever villages or towns or countryside he entered, they laid the sick in the marketplaces and begged him that they might touch only the tassel on his cloak; and as many as touched it were healed.

387   *As circumstances suggest, one of the following responsorial psalms may be sung or said, or some other suitable song.*

R. *Lord, you have preserved my life from destruction.*

Isaiah 38
Once I said,
"In the noontime of life I must depart!
To the gates of the nether world I shall be consigned
for the rest of my years." **R.**

I said, "I shall see the Lord no more
in the land of the living.
No longer shall I behold my fellow men
among those who dwell in the world." **R.**

My dwelling, like a shepherd's tent,

is struck down and borne away from me;
You have folded up my life, like a weaver
who severs the last thread. *R.*

Those live whom the LORD protects;
yours . . . the life of my spirit.
You have given me health and life. *R.*

Psalm 102:2–3, 24–25

R. (v. 2) O Lord, hear my prayer, and let my cry come to you.

388   *As circumstances suggest, the minister may give those present a
brief explanation of the biblical text, so that they may understand through
faith the meaning of the celebration.*

INTERCESSIONS

389   *The intercessions are then said. The minister introduces them and
an assisting minister or one of those present announces the intentions.
From the following intentions those best suited to the occasion may be
used or adapted, or other intentions that apply to those who are sick and
to the particular circumstances may be composed.*

The minister says:

The Lord Jesus loves our brothers and sisters who are ill.
With trust let us pray to him that he will comfort them with
his grace, saying:

R. Lord, give those who are sick the comfort of your presence.

Assisting minister:

Lord Jesus, you came as healer of body and of spirit, in order
to cure all our ills. *R.*

Assisting minister:

You were a man of suffering, but it was our infirmities that you bore, our sufferings that you endured. **R.**

Assisting minister:

You chose to be like us in all things, in order to assure us of your compassion. **R.**

Assisting minister:

You experienced the weakness of the flesh in order to deliver us from evil. **R.**

Assisting minister:

At the foot of the cross your Mother stood as companion in your sufferings, and in your tender care you gave her to us as our Mother. **R.**

Assisting minister:

It is your wish that in our own flesh we should fill up what is wanting in your sufferings for the sake of your Body, the Church. **R.**

390   *Instead of the intercessions or in addition to them, one of the following litanies taken from Pastoral Care of the Sick, nos. 245 and 138 may be used.*

Minister:

You bore our weakness and carried our sorrows:
Lord, have mercy.

R. *Lord, have mercy.*

Minister:

You felt compassion for the crowd, and went about doing good and healing the sick: Christ, have mercy.

R. *Christ, have mercy.*

Minister:

You commanded your apostles to lay their hands on the sick in your name: Lord, have mercy.

R. *Lord, have mercy.*

391   Or:

The minister says:

Let us pray to God for our brothers and sisters and for all those who devote themselves to caring for them.

Assisting minister:

Bless **N.** and **N.** and fill them with new hope and strength: Lord, have mercy.

R. *Lord, have mercy.*

Assisting minister:

Relieve their pain: Lord, have mercy. **R.**

Assisting minister:

Free them from sin and do not let them give way to temptation: Lord, have mercy. **R.**

Assisting minister:

Sustain all the sick with your power: Lord, have mercy. **R.**

Assisting minister:

Assist all who care for the sick: Lord, have mercy. **R.**

Assisting minister:

Give life and health to our brothers and sisters on whom we lay our hands in your name: Lord, have mercy. **R.**

PRAYER OF BLESSING

394   A lay minister traces the sign of the cross on the forehead of each sick person and says the following prayer of blessing.

Lord, our God,
who watch over your creatures with unfailing care,
keep us in the safe embrace of your love.
With your strong right hand raise up your servants
    (*N.* and *N.*)
and give them the strength of your own power.
Minister to them and heal their illnesses,
so that they may have from you the help they long for.

Through Christ our Lord.

R. *Amen.*

395   Or, for one sick person:

Lord and Father, almighty and eternal God,
by your blessing you give us strength and support
    in our frailty:
turn with kindness toward this your servant *N.*
Free him/her from all illness and restore him/her to health,
so that in the sure knowledge of your goodness
he/she will gratefully bless your holy name.

Through Christ our Lord.

R. *Amen.*

396   After the prayer of blessing the minister invites all present to pray for the protection of the Blessed Virgin. They may do so by singing or reciting a Marian antiphon, for example, We turn to you for protection (Sub tuum praesidium) *or* Hail, Holy Queen.

Concluding Rite

398   A lay minister invokes the Lord's blessing on the sick and all present by signing himself or herself with the sign of the cross and saying:

May the Lord Jesus Christ,
who went about doing good and healing the sick,
grant that we may have good health
and be enriched by his blessings.

R. *Amen.*

B. ORDER FOR THE BLESSING OF CHILDREN

399   For the blessing of sick children, the texts already given are to be adapted to the children's level, but special intercessions are provided here and a special prayer of blessing.

Intercessions

400   To the following intentions others may be added that apply to the condition of the sick children and to the particular circumstances.

The minister says:

The Lord Jesus loved and cherished the little ones with a special love. Let us, then, pray to him for these sick children, saying:

R. *Lord, keep them in all their ways.*

Or:

R. *Lord, hear our prayer.*

Assisting minister:

Lord Jesus, you called the little children to come to you and said that the kingdom of heaven belongs to such as these; listen with mercy to our prayers for these children. (For this we pray:) **R.**

Assisting minister:

You revealed the mysteries of the kingdom of heaven, not to the wise of this world, but to little children; give these children the proof of your love. (For this we pray:) **R.**

Assisting minister:

You praised the children who cried out their Hosannas on the eve of your Passion; strengthen these children and their parents with your holy comfort. (For this we pray:) **R.**

Assisting minister:

You charged your disciples to take care of the sick; stand at the side of all those who so gladly devote themselves to restoring the health of these children. (For this we pray:) **R.**

PRAYER OF BLESSING

402   A lay minister, and particularly a mother or father when blessing a sick child, traces the sign of the cross on each child's forehead and then says the following prayer of blessing.

Father of mercy and God of all consolation,
you show tender care for all your creatures
and give health of soul and body.
Raise up these children
   (*or* this child *or* the son/daughter you have given us)
   from their (his/her) sickness.
Then, growing in wisdom and grace in your sight and ours,
they (he/she) will serve you all the days of their (his/her) life
in uprightness and holiness
and offer the thanksgiving due to your mercy.

Through Christ our Lord.
R. *Amen.*

C. SHORTER RITE

403   The minister says:

Our help is in the name of the Lord.

All reply:

Who made heaven and earth.

404   One of those present or the minister reads a text of sacred Scripture, for example:

2 Corinthians 1:3–4

Blessed be the God and Father of our Lord Jesus Christ, the Father of compassion and God of all encouragement, who encourages us in our every affliction, so that we may be able to encourage those who are in any affliction with the encouragement with which we ourselves are encouraged by God.

Matthew 11:28–29

Jesus said, "Come to me, all you who labor and are burdened, and I will give you rest. Take my yoke upon you and learn from me, for I am meek and humble of heart; and you will find rest for yourselves."

405   As circumstances suggest . . . a lay minister may trace the sign of the cross on the sick person's forehead while saying the prayer.

Lord and Father, almighty and eternal God,
by your blessing you give us strength and support
    in our frailty:
turn with kindness toward your servant, **N.**
Free him/her from all illness and restore him/her to health,
so that in the sure knowledge of your goodness
he/she will gratefully bless your holy name.

Through Christ our Lord.

R. *Amen.*

Order for the Blessing of a Person Suffering from Addiction or from Substance Abuse

INTRODUCTION

407   Addiction to alcohol, drugs, and other controlled substances causes great disruption in the life of an individual and his or her family. This blessing is intended to strengthen the addicted person in the struggle to overcome addiction and also to assist his or her family and friends.

408   This blessing may also be used for individuals who, although not addicted, abuse alcohol or drugs and wish the assistance of God's blessing in their struggle.

409   Ministers should be aware of the spiritual needs of a person suffering from addiction or substance abuse, and to this end the pastoral guidance on the care of the sick and rites of *Pastoral Care of the Sick* will be helpful.

410   If the recovery process is slow or is marked by relapses, the blessing may be repeated when pastorally appropriate.

411   These orders may be used by a priest or a deacon, and also by a layperson, who follows the rites and prayers designated for a lay minister.

A. ORDER OF BLESSING

INTRODUCTORY RITES

412   When the community has gathered, a suitable song may be sung. After the singing, the minister says:

In the name of the Father, and of the Son, and of the Holy Spirit.

All make the sign of the cross and reply:

Amen.

414   A lay minister greets those present in the following words:

Let us praise God our creator, who gives us courage and strength, now and for ever.

R. *Amen.*

415   In the following or similar words, the minister prepares those present for the blessing.

God created the world and all things in it and entrusted them into our hands that we might use them for our good and for the building up of the Church and human society. Today we pray for **N.**, that God may strengthen him/her in his/her weakness and restore him/her to the freedom of God's children. We pray also for ourselves that we may encourage and support him/her in the days ahead.

Reading of the Word of God

416   A reader, another person present, or the minister reads a text of sacred Scripture.

Brothers and sisters, listen to the words of the second letter of Paul to the Corinthians: 4:6–9

We are afflicted, but not crushed.

For God who said, "Let light shine out of darkness," has shone in our hearts to bring to light the knowledge of the glory of God on the face of Jesus Christ.

But we hold this treasure in earthen vessels, that the surpassing power may be of God and not from us. We are afflicted in every way, but not constrained; perplexed, but not driven to despair; persecuted, but not abandoned; struck down, but not destroyed.

417   Or:

Isaiah 63:7–9—He has favored us according to his mercy.

Romans 8:18–25—I consider the sufferings of the present to be as nothing compared with the glory to be revealed in us.

Matthew 15:21–28—Woman, you have great faith.

418   As circumstances suggest, one of the following responsorial psalms may be sung or said, or some other suitable song.

***R.** Our help is from the Lord who made heaven and earth.*

Psalm 121

I lift up my eyes toward the mountains;
whence shall help come to me?
My help is from the Lord
who made heaven and earth. **R.**

May he not suffer your foot to slip;
may he slumber not who guards you:
Indeed he neither slumbers nor sleeps,
the guardian of Israel. **R.**

The LORD is your guardian; the LORD is your shade;
he is beside you at your right hand.
The sun shall not harm you by day,
nor the moon by night. **R.**

The LORD will guard you from all evil;
he will guard your life.
The LORD will guard your coming and your going,
both now and forever. **R.**

Psalm 130.1–2, 3–4, 5–6, 7–8

R. *(v. 5) My soul trusts in the Lord.*

419   As circumstances suggest, the minister may give those present a brief explanation of the biblical text, so that they may understand through faith the meaning of the celebration.

INTERCESSIONS

420   The intercessions are then said. The minister introduces them and an assisting minister or one of those present announces the intentions. From the following those best suited to the occasion may be used or adapted, or other intentions that apply to the particular circumstances may be composed.

The minister says:

Our God gives us life and constantly calls us to new life; let us pray to God with confidence.

R. *Lord, hear our prayer.*

Assisting minister:

For those addicted to alcohol/drugs, that God may be their strength and support, we pray. *R.*

Assisting minister:

For **N.**, bound by the chains of addiction/substance abuse, that we encourage and assist him/her in his/her struggle, we pray. *R.*

Assisting minister:

For **N.**, that he/she may trust in the mercy of God through whom all things are possible, we pray. *R.*

Assisting minister:

For the family and friends of **N.,** that with faith and patience they show him/her their love, we pray. *R.*

Assisting minister:

For the Church, that it may always be attentive to those in need, we pray. *R.*

421   After the intercessions the minister, in the following or similar words, invites all present to sing or say the Lord's Prayer.

Let us pray to our merciful God as Jesus taught us:

All:

Our Father . . .

Prayer of Blessing

422   A lay minister says the prayer with hands joined.

A   *For addiction*

God of mercy,
we bless you in the name of your Son, Jesus Christ,
who ministered to all who came to him.
Give your strength to *N.,* your servant,
bound by the chains of addiction.
Enfold him/her in your love
and restore him/her to the freedom of God's children.

Lord,
look with compassion on all those
who have lost their health and freedom.
Restore to them the assurance of your unfailing mercy,
and strengthen them in the work of recovery.

To those who care for them,
grant patient understanding and a love that perseveres.

Through Christ our Lord.

R. *Amen.*

B   *For substance abuse*

God of mercy,
we bless you in the name of your Son, Jesus Christ,
who ministered to all who came to him.
Give your strength to *N.,* your servant,
enfold him/her in your love
and restore him/her to the freedom of God's children.

Lord,
look with compassion on all those
who have lost their health and freedom.
Restore to them the assurance of your unfailing mercy,
strengthen them in the work of recovery,
and help them to resist all temptation.

To those who care for them,
grant patient understanding and a love that perseveres.

Through Christ our Lord.

R. *Amen.*

*As circumstances suggest, the minister in silence may sprinkle the person
with holy water.*

CONCLUDING RITE

*424 A lay minister concludes the rite by signing himself or herself with
the sign of the cross and saying:*

May our all-merciful God, Father, Son, and Holy Spirit, bless
us and embrace us in love for ever.

R. *Amen.*

425 It is preferable to end the celebration with a suitable song.

B. SHORTER RITE

426 All make the sign of the cross as the minister says:

Our help is in the name of the Lord.

All reply:

Who made heaven and earth.

427   *One of those present or the minister reads a text of sacred Scripture, for example:*

Brothers and sisters, listen to the words of the second letter of Paul to the Corinthians: 4:6–9

We are afflicted, but not crushed.

For God who said, "Let light shine out of darkness," has shone in our hearts to bring to light the knowledge of the glory of God on the face of Jesus Christ.

But we hold this treasure in earthen vessels, that the surpassing power may be of God and not from us. We are afflicted in every way, but not constrained; perplexed, but not driven to despair; persecuted, but not abandoned; struck down, but not destroyed.

428   *Or:*

Isaiah 63:7–9—He has favored us according to his mercy.

Matthew 15:21–28—Woman, you have great faith.

429   *A lay minister says the prayer with hands joined.*

A   *For addiction*

God of mercy,
we bless you in the name of your Son, Jesus Christ,
who ministered to all who came to him.
Give your strength to **N.**, your servant,
bound by the chains of addiction.
Enfold him/her in your love
and restore him/her to the freedom of God's children.

Lord,
look with compassion on all those
who have lost their health and freedom.
Restore to them the assurance of your unfailing mercy,
and strengthen them in the work of recovery.

To those who care for them,
grant patient understanding and a love that perseveres.

Through Christ our Lord.
R. *Amen.*

B   *For substance abuse*

God of mercy,
we bless you in the name of your Son, Jesus Christ,
who ministered to all who came to him.
Give your strength to **N.**, your servant,
enfold him/her in your love
and restore him/her to the freedom of God's children.

Lord,
look with compassion on all those
who have lost their health and freedom.
Restore to them the assurance of your unfailing mercy,
strengthen them in the work of recovery,
and help them to resist all temptation.

To those who care for them,
grant patient understanding and a love that perseveres.

Through Christ our Lord.
R. *Amen.*

Order for the Blessing of a Victim of Crime or Oppression

INTRODUCTION

430   The personal experience of a crime, political oppression, or social oppression can be traumatic and not easily forgotten. A victim often needs the assistance of others, and no less that of God, in dealing with this experience.

431   This blessing is intended to assist the victim and help him or her come to a state of tranquility and peace.

432   These orders may be used by a priest or a deacon, and also by a layperson, who follows the rites and prayers designated for a lay minister.

A. ORDER OF BLESSING

INTRODUCTORY RITES

*433   When the community has gathered, a suitable song may be sung.
After the singing, the minister says:*

In the name of the Father, and of the Son, and of the Holy Spirit.
All make the sign of the cross and reply:

Amen.

435   A lay minister greets those present in the following words:

May the Lord grant us peace, now and for ever.

R. *Amen.*

*436   In the following or similar words, the minister prepares those
present for the blessing.*

Throughout history God has manifested his love and care for
those who have suffered from violence, hatred, and oppression.
We commend **N.** to the healing mercy of God who binds up
all our wounds and enfolds us in his gentle care.

READING OF THE WORD OF GOD

*437   A reader, another person present, or the minister reads a text of
sacred Scripture.*

**Brothers and sisters, listen to the words of
the holy gospel according to Matthew:**   10:28–33
Do not fear.

Jesus said to his disciples: "Do not be afraid of those who kill
the body but cannot kill the soul; rather, be afraid of the one
who can destroy both soul and body in Gehenna. Are not two
sparrows sold for a small coin? Yet not one of them falls to the
ground without your Father's knowledge. Even all the hairs of

your head are counted. So do not be afraid; you are worth more than many sparrows. Everyone who acknowledges me before others I will acknowledge before my heavenly Father. But whoever denies me before others, I will deny before my heavenly Father."

438   Or:

Isaiah 59:6b–8, 15–18—The Lord is appalled by evil and injustice.

Job 3:1–26—Lamentation of Job.

Lamentations 3:1–24—I am one who knows affliction.

Lamentations 3:49–59—When I called, you came to my aid.

Micah 4:1–4—Every person shall sit undisturbed.

Matthew 5:1–10—The beatitudes.

Matthew 5:43–48—Love your enemies, pray for those who persecute you.

Luke 10:25–37—The good Samaritan.

439   As circumstances suggest, one of the following responsorial psalms may be sung, or some other suitable song.

R. *The Lord is my strength and my salvation.*

Psalm 140

Deliver me, O Lord, from evil men;
preserve me from violent men,
From those who devise evil in their hearts,
and stir up wars every day. **R.**

Save me, O Lord, from the hands of the wicked;
preserve me from violent men
Who plan to trip up my feet—
the proud who have hidden a trap for me;
They have spread cords for a net;
by the wayside they have laid snares for me. **R.**

Grant not, O LORD, the desires of the wicked;
further not their plans.
Those who surround me lift up their heads;
may the mischief which they threaten overwhelm them. **R.**

I know that the LORD renders
justice to the afflicted, judgment to the poor.
Surely the just shall give thanks to your name;
the upright shall dwell in your presence. **R.**

Psalm 142:2–3, 4b–5, 6–7
R. *(v. 6) You, O Lord, are my refuge.*

Psalm 31:2–3a, 4–5, 15–16, 24–25
R. *(v. 6) Into your hands I commend my spirit.*

*440   As circumstances suggest, the minister may give those present a
brief explanation of the biblical text, so that they may understand through
faith the meaning of the celebration.*

INTERCESSIONS

*441   The intercessions are then said. The minister introduces them and
an assisting minister or one of those present announces the intentions.
From the following those best suited to the occasion may be used or
adapted, or other intentions that apply to the particular circumstances
may be composed.*

The minister says:
Let us pray to the Lord God, the defender of the
weak and powerless, who delivered our ancestors from harm.

R. *Deliver us from evil, O Lord.*

Assisting minister:

For **N.,** that he/she may be freed from pain and fear, we pray to the Lord. **R.**

Assisting minister:

For all who are victims of crime/oppression, we pray to the Lord. **R.**

Assisting minister:

For an end to all acts of violence and hatred, we pray to the Lord. **R.**

Assisting minister:

For those who harm others, that they may change their lives and turn to God, we pray to the Lord. **R.**

442   After the intercessions the minister, in the following or similar words, invites all present to sing or say the Lord's Prayer.

The Lord heals our wounds and strengthens us in our weakness; let us pray as Christ has taught us:

All:

Our Father . . .

PRAYER OF BLESSING

443   A lay minister says the prayer with hands joined.

Lord God,
your own Son was delivered into the hands of the wicked,
yet he prayed for his persecutors
and overcame hatred with the blood of the cross.
Relieve the suffering of **N.**;
grant him/her peace of mind
and a renewed faith in your protection and care.

Protect us all from the violence of others,
keep us safe from the weapons of hate,
and restore to us tranquility and peace.

Through Christ our Lord.
R. Amen.

As circumstances suggest, the minister in silence may sprinkle the person with holy water.

CONCLUDING RITE

445   A lay minister concludes the rite by signing himself or herself with the Sign of the Cross and saying:

May God bless us with his mercy,
strengthen us with his love,
and enable us to walk in charity and peace.

R. *Amen.*

446   It is preferable to end the celebration with a suitable song.

B. SHORTER RITE

447 *All make the sign of the cross as the minister says:*

Our help is in the name of the Lord.

All reply:

Who made heaven and earth.

448   *One of those present or the minister reads a text of sacred Scripture, for example:*

Brothers and sisters, listen to the words of the holy gospel according to Matthew: 10:28–33

Do not fear.

Jesus said to his disciples: "Do not be afraid of those who kill the body but cannot kill the soul; rather, be afraid of the one who can destroy both soul and body in Gehenna. Are not two sparrows sold for a small coin? Yet not one of them falls to the ground without your Father's knowledge. Even all the hairs of your head are counted. So do not be afraid; you are worth more than many sparrows. Everyone who acknowledges me before others I will acknowledge before my heavenly Father. But whoever denies me before others, I will deny before my heavenly Father."

449   *Or:*

Isaiah 59:6b–8, 15–18—The Lord is appalled by evil and injustice.

Job 3:1–26—Lamentation of Job.

Lamentations 3:1–24—I am a man who knows affliction.

Lamentations 3:49–59—When I called, you came to my aid.

Matthew 5:1–10—The beatitudes.

Luke 10:25–37—The good Samaritan.

Lord God,
your own Son was delivered into the hands of the wicked
yet he prayed for his persecutors
and overcame hatred with the blood of the cross.
Relieve the suffering of **N.**;
grant him/her peace of mind
and a renewed faith in your protection and care.

Protect us all from the violence of others,
keep us safe from the weapons of hate,
and restore to us tranquility and peace.

Through Christ our Lord.

R. *Amen.*

Order for the Blessing of Parents after a Miscarriage

INTRODUCTION

279   In times of death and grief the Christian turns to the Lord for consolation and strength. This is especially true when a child dies before birth. This blessing is provided to assist the parents in their grief and console them with the blessing of God.

280   The minister should be attentive to the needs of the parents and other family members and to this end the introduction to the *Order of Christian Funerals,* Part II: Funeral Rites for Children will be helpful.

281   These orders may be used by a priest or deacon, and also by a layperson who follows the rites and prayers designated for a lay minister.

A. ORDER OF BLESSING

INTRODUCTORY RITES

282   When the community has gathered, a suitable song may be sung. The minister says:

In the name of the Father, and of the Son, and of the Holy Spirit.

All make the sign of the cross and reply:

Amen.

284   A lay minister greets those present in the following words:

Let us praise the Father of mercies, the God of all consolation. Blessed be God for ever.

R. *Blessed be God for ever.*

285   In the following or similar words, the minister prepares those present for the blessing.

For those who trust in God,
in the pain of sorrow there is consolation,
in the face of despair there is hope,
in the midst of death there is life.
N. and **N.**, as we mourn the death of your child
we place ourselves in the hands of God
and ask for strength, for healing, and for love.

Reading of the Word of God

286   A reader, another person present, or the minister reads a text of sacred Scripture.

Brothers and sisters, listen to the words of the book of Lamentations: 3:17–26

Hope in the Lord.
My soul is deprived of peace,
I have forgotten what happiness is;
I tell myself my future is lost,
all that I hoped for from the Lord.
The thought of my homeless poverty
is wormwood and gall;
Remembering it over and over
leaves my soul downcast within me.
But I will call this to mind,
as my reason to have hope:
The favors of the Lord are not exhausted,
his mercies are not spent;
They are renewed each morning,
so great is his faithfulness.
My portion is the Lord, says my soul;
therefore will I hope in him.
Good is the Lord to one who waits for him,
to the soul that seeks him;
It is good to hope in silence
for the saving help of the Lord.

287   Or:

Isaiah 49:8–13—In a time of favor I answer you, on the day of salvation I help you.

Romans 8:18–27—In hope we were saved.

Romans 8:26–31—If God is for us, who can be against us?

Colossians 1:9–12—We have been praying for you unceasingly.

Hebrews 5:7–10—Christ intercedes for us.

Luke 22:39–46—Agony in the garden.

288   As circumstances suggest, one of the following responsorial psalms may be sung, or some other suitable song.

R. *To you, O Lord, I lift up my soul.*

Psalm 25

Your ways, O LORD, make known to me;
teach me your paths,
Guide me in your truth and teach me,
for you are God my savior,
and for you I wait all the day. **R.**

Remember that your compassion, O LORD,
and your kindness are from of old.
The sins of my youth and my frailties remember not;
in your kindness remember me
because of your goodness, O LORD. **R.**

Look toward me, and have pity on me,
for I am alone and afflicted.
Relieve the troubles of my heart,
and bring me out of my distress. **R.**

Preserve my life, and rescue me;
let me not be put to shame, for I take refuge in you.
Let integrity and uprightness preserve me,
because I wait for you, O Lord. **R.**

Psalm 143:1, 5–6, 8, 10

R. *(v. 1) O Lord, hear my prayer.*

*289   As circumstances suggest, the minister may give those present a
brief explanation of the biblical text, so that they may understand through
faith the meaning of the celebration.*

INTERCESSIONS

*290   The intercessions are then said. The minister introduces them and
an assisting minister or one of those present announces the intentions.
From the following those best suited to the occasion may be used or
adapted, or other intentions that apply to the particular circumstances
may be composed.*

The minister says:

Let us pray to God who throughout the ages has heard the
cries of parents.

R. *Lord, hear our prayer.*

Assisting minister:

For **N.** and **N.**, who know the pain of grief, that they may be
comforted, we pray. **R.**

Assisting minister:

For this family, that it may find new hope in the midst of
suffering, we pray. **R.**

Assisting minister:

For these parents, that they may learn from the example of Mary, who grieved by the cross of her Son, we pray. **R.**

Assisting minister:

For all who have suffered the loss of a child, that Christ may be their support, we pray. **R.**

291   *After the intercessions the minister, in the following or similar words, invites all present to sing or say the Lord's Prayer.*

Let us pray to the God of consolation and hope, as Christ has taught us:

All:

Our Father . . .

PRAYER OF BLESSING

292   *A lay minister says the prayer with hands joined.*

Compassionate God,
soothe the hearts of **N.** and **N.**,
and grant that through the prayers of Mary,
who grieved by the cross of her Son,
you may enlighten their faith,
give hope to their hearts,
and peace to their lives.

Lord,
grant mercy to all the members of this family
and comfort them with the hope
that one day we will all live with you,
with your Son Jesus Christ, and the Holy Spirit,
for ever and ever.
R. *Amen.*

293   Or:

Lord,
God of all creation
we bless and thank you for your tender care.
Receive this life you created in love
and comfort your faithful people in their time of loss
with the assurance of your unfailing mercy.

Through Christ our Lord.

R. *Amen.*

*As circumstances suggest, the minister in silence may sprinkle the parents
with holy water.*

CONCLUDING RITE

*295   A lay minister concludes the rite by signing himself or herself with
the sign of the cross and saying:*

May God give us peace in our sorrow,
consolation in our grief,
and strength to accept his will in all things.

R. *Amen.*

296   It is preferable to end the celebration with a suitable song.

B. SHORTER RITE

297 *All make the sign of the cross as the minister says:*

Our help is in the name of the Lord.

All reply:

Who made heaven and earth.

298 *One of those present or the minister reads a text of sacred Scripture, for example:*

Brothers and sisters, listen to the words of the book of Lamentations: 3:17–26

Hope in the Lord.

My soul is deprived of peace,
I have forgotten what happiness is;
I tell myself my future is lost,
all that I hoped for from the Lord.
The thought of my homeless poverty
is wormwood and gall;
Remembering it over and over
leaves my soul downcast within me.
But I will call this to mind,
as my reason to have hope:
The favors of the LORD are not exhausted,
his mercies are not spent;
They are renewed each morning,
so great is his faithfulness.
My portion is the LORD, says my soul;
therefore will I hope in him.
Good is the LORD to one who waits for him,
to the soul that seeks him;
It is good to hope in silence
for the saving help of the LORD.

299   Or:

Romans 8:26–31—If God is for us, who can be against us?

Colossians 1:9–12—We have been praying for you unceasingly.

300   A lay minister says the prayer with hands joined.

Compassionate God,
soothe the hearts of **N.** and **N.**,
and grant that through the prayers of Mary,
who grieved by the cross of her Son,
you may enlighten their faith,
give hope to their hearts,
and peace to their lives.

Lord,
grant mercy to all the members of this family
and comfort them with the hope
that one day we will all live with you,
with your Son Jesus Christ, and the Holy Spirit,
for ever and ever.

R. *Amen.*

301   Or:

Lord,
God of all creation,
we bless and thank you for your tender care.
Receive this life you created in love
and comfort your faithful people in their time of loss
with the assurance of your unfailing mercy.

Through Christ our Lord.

R. *Amen.*

Pastoral Care of the Sick

INTRODUCTION

Lord, your friend is sick.

42　　The rites in Part I of *Pastoral Care of the Sick: Rites of Anointing and Viaticum* are used by the Church to comfort the sick in time of anxiety, to encourage them to fight against illness, and perhaps to restore them to health. These rites are distinct from those in the second part of this book, which are provided to comfort and strengthen a Christian in the passage from this life.

43　　The concern that Christ showed for the bodily and spiritual welfare of those who are ill is continued by the Church in its ministry to the sick. This ministry is the common responsibility of all Christians, who should visit the sick, remember them in prayer, and celebrate the sacraments with them. The family and friends of the sick, doctors and others who care for them, and Priests with pastoral responsibilities have a particular share in this ministry of comfort. Through words of encouragement and faith they can help the sick to unite themselves with the sufferings of Christ for the good of God's people.

　　Remembrance of the sick is especially appropriate at common worship on the Lord's Day, during the Universal Prayer at Mass and in the intercessions at Morning Prayer and Evening Prayer. Family members and those who are dedicated to the care of the sick should be remembered on these occasions as well.

44　　Priests have the special task of preparing the sick to celebrate the Sacrament of Penance (individually or in a communal celebration), to receive the Eucharist frequently if their condition permits, and to celebrate the Sacrament of Anointing at the appropriate time. During this preparation it will be especially helpful if the sick person, the Priest, and the family become accustomed to praying together. The Priest should provide leadership to those who assist him in the care of the sick, especially Deacons and other ministers of the Eucharist.

The words "Priest," "Deacon," and "minister" are used advisedly. Only in those rites which must be celebrated by a Priest is the word "Priest" used in the rubrics (that is, the Sacrament of Penance, the Sacrament of the Anointing of the Sick, the celebration of Viaticum within Mass). Whenever it is clear that, in the absence of a Priest, a Deacon may preside at a particular rite, the words "Priest or Deacon" are used in the rubrics. Whenever another minister is permitted to celebrate a rite in the absence of a Priest or Deacon, the word "minister" is used in the rubrics, even though in many cases the rite will be celebrated by a Priest or Deacon.

45   The pastoral care of the sick should be suited to the nature and length of the illness. An illness of short duration in which the full recovery of health is a possibility requires a more intensive ministry, whereas illness of a longer duration which may be a prelude to death requires a more extensive ministry. An awareness of the attitudes and emotional states which these different situations engender in the sick is indispensable to the development of an appropriate ministry.

Visits to the Sick

46   Those who visit the sick should help them to pray, sharing with them the word of God proclaimed in the assembly from which their sickness has separated them. As the occasion permits, prayer drawn from the psalms or from other prayers or litanies may be added to the word of God. Care should be taken to prepare for a future visit during which the sick will receive the Eucharist.

Visits to a Sick Child

47   What has already been said about visiting the sick and praying with them (see no. 46) applies also in visits to a sick child. Every effort should be made to know the child and to accommodate the care in keeping with the age and comprehension of the child. In these circumstances the minister should also be particularly concerned to help the child's family.

48   If it is appropriate, the Priest may discuss with the parents the possibility of preparing and celebrating with the child the Sacraments of Initiation (Baptism, Confirmation, Eucharist). The Priest may baptize and confirm the child (see *Rite of Confirmation,* no. 7b). To complete the process of Initiation, the child should also receive first Communion. (If the child is a proper subject for Confirmation, then he or she may receive first Communion in accordance with the practice of the Church.) There is no reason to delay this, especially if the illness is likely to be a long one.

49   Throughout the illness the minister should ensure that the child receives Communion frequently, making whatever adaptations seem necessary in the rite for Communion of the sick (Chapter III).

50   The child is to be anointed if he or she has sufficient use of reason to be strengthened by the Sacrament of Anointing. The rites provided (Chapter IV) are to be used and adapted.

Communion of the Sick

51   Because the sick are prevented from celebrating the Eucharist with the rest of the community, the most important visits are those during which they receive Holy Communion. In receiving the Body and Blood of Christ, the sick are united sacramentally to the Lord and are reunited with the Eucharistic community from which illness has separated them.

Anointing of the Sick

52   The Priest should be especially concerned for those whose health has been seriously impaired by illness or old age. He will offer them a new sign of hope: the laying on of hands and the Anointing of the Sick accompanied by the prayer of faith (James 5:14). Those who receive this sacrament in the faith of the Church will find it a true sign of comfort and support in time of trial. It will work to overcome the sickness, if this is God's will.

53   Some types of mental sickness are now classified as serious. Those who are judged to have a serious mental illness and who would be strengthened by the sacrament may be anointed (see no. 5). The anointing may be repeated in accordance with the conditions for other kinds of serious illness (see no. 9).

Visits to the Sick

INTRODUCTION

I was sick, and you visited me.

54   The prayers contained in this chapter follow the common pattern of reading, response, prayer, and blessing. This pattern is provided as an example of what can be done and may be adapted as necessary. The minister may wish to invite those present to prepare for the reading from Scripture, perhaps by a brief introduction or through a moment of silence. The laying on of hands may be added by the Priest, if appropriate, after the blessing is given.

55   The sick should be encouraged to pray when they are alone or with their families, friends, or those who care for them. Their prayer should be drawn primarily from Scripture. The sick person and others may help to plan the celebration, for example, by choosing the prayers and readings. Those making these choices should keep in mind the condition of the sick person.

    The passages found in this chapter and those included in Part III speak of the mystery of human suffering in the words, works, and life of Christ. Occasionally, for example, on the Lord's Day, the sick may feel more involved in the worship of the community from which they are separated if the readings used are those assigned for that day in the Lectionary. Prayers may also be drawn from the psalms or from other prayers or litanies. The sick should be helped in making this form of prayer, and the minister should always be ready to pray with them.

56   The minister should encourage the sick person to offer his or her sufferings in union with Christ and to join in prayer for the Church and the world. Some examples of particular intentions which may be suggested to the sick person are: for peace in the world; for a deepening of the life of the Spirit in the local Church; for the pope and the bishops; for people suffering in a particular disaster.

READING

57   The word of God is proclaimed by one of those present or by the minister. An appropriate reading from Part III or one of the following readings may be used:

A   *Acts of the Apostles 3:1–10*

In the name of Jesus and the power of his Church, there is salvation—even liberation from sickness.

B   *Matthew 8:14–17*

Jesus fulfills the prophetic figure of the servant of God taking upon himself and relieving the sufferings of God's people.

RESPONSE

58   A brief period of silence may be observed after the reading of the word of God. An appropriate psalm from Part III or one of the following psalms may be used:

A   *Psalm 102*

R. *O Lord, hear my prayer and let my cry come to you.*

O Lord, hear my prayer,
   and let my cry come to you.
Hide not your face from me
   in the day of my distress.
Incline your ear to me;
   in the day when I call, answer me speedily. **R.**

He has broken down my strength in the way;
  he has cut short my days. I say: O my God,
Take me not hence in the midst of my days;
  through all generations your years endure. **R.**

Of old you established the earth,
  and the heavens are the work of your hands.
They shall perish, but you remain
  though all of them grow old like a garment.
Like clothing you change them, and they are changed,
  but you are the same, and your years have no end. **R.**

Let this be written for the generation to come,
  and let his future creatures praise the Lord:
"The Lord looked down from his holy height,
  from heaven he beheld the earth,
To hear the groaning of the prisoners,
  to release those doomed to die." **R.**

B   *Psalm 27*

R. *The Lord is my light and my salvation.*

The Lord is my light and my salvation;
  whom should I fear?
The Lord is my life's refuge;
  of whom should I be afraid? **R.**

One thing I ask of the Lord;
  this I seek:
To dwell in the house of the Lord
  all the days of my life
That I may gaze on the loveliness of the Lord
  and contemplate his temple. **R.**

For he will hide me in his abode
in the day of trouble,
He will conceal me in the shelter of his tent,
he will set me high upon a rock. **R.**

The minister may then give a brief explanation of the reading, applying it to the needs of the sick person and those who are looking after him or her.

THE LORD'S PRAYER

59   *The minister introduces the Lord's Prayer in these or similar words:*

Now let us offer together the prayer our Lord Jesus Christ taught us:

All say:
Our Father . . .

CONCLUDING PRAYER

60   *The minister says a concluding prayer. One of the following may be used:*

A

O God, who willed that our infirmities
be borne by your Only Begotten Son
to show the value of human suffering,
listen in kindness to our prayers
for our brothers and sisters who are sick;
grant that all who are oppressed by pain, distress
or other afflictions

may know that they are chosen
among those proclaimed blessed
and are united to Christ
in his suffering for the salvation of the world.
Through Christ our Lord.

R. *Amen.*

B

Almighty ever-living God, eternal health of believers,
hear our prayers for your servants who are sick:
grant them, we implore you, your merciful help,
so that, with their health restored,
they may give you thanks in the midst of your Church.
Through Christ our Lord.

R. *Amen.*

C

All-powerful and ever-living God,
we find security in your forgiveness.
Give us serenity and peace of mind;
may we rejoice in your gifts of kindness
and use them always for your glory and our good.

We ask this in the name of Jesus the Lord.

R. *Amen.*

BLESSING

61   The minister may give a blessing. One of the following may be used:

A

All praise and glory is yours, Lord our God,
for you have called us to serve you in love.
Bless **N.**
so that he/she may bear this illness
in union with your Son's obedient suffering.
Restore him/her to health,
and lead him/her to glory.

Through Christ our Lord.

R. *Amen.*

B

For an elderly person

All praise and glory are yours, Lord our God,
for you have called us to serve you in love.
Bless all who have grown old in your service
and give **N.** strength and courage
to continue to follow Jesus your Son.

Through Christ our Lord.

R. *Amen.*

A minister who is not a Priest or Deacon invokes God's blessing and makes the Sign of the Cross on himself or herself, while saying:

May the Lord bless us,
protect us from all evil,
and bring us to everlasting life.

R. *Amen.*

The minister may then trace the Sign of the Cross on the sick person's forehead.

Visits to a Sick Child

INTRODUCTION

Let the children come to me; do not keep them back from me.

62   The following readings, prayers, and blessings will help the minister to pray with sick children and their families. They are provided as an example of what can be done and may be adapted as necessary. The minister may wish to invite those present to prepare for the reading from Scripture, perhaps by a brief introduction or through a moment of silence.

63   If the child does not already know the minister, the latter should seek to establish a friendly and easy relationship with the child. Therefore, the greeting which begins the visit should be an informal one.

64   The minister should help sick children to understand that the sick are very special in the eyes of God because they are suffering as Christ suffered and because they can offer their sufferings for the salvation of the world.

65   In praying with the sick child the minister chooses, together with the child and the family if possible, suitable elements of common prayer in the form of a brief Liturgy of the Word. This may consist of a reading from Scripture, simple one-line prayers taken from Scripture which can be repeated by the child, other familiar prayers such as the Lord's Prayer, the Hail Mary, litanies, or a simple form of the Universal Prayer. The laying on of hands may be added by the Priest, if appropriate, after the child has been blessed.

READING

66   One of the following readings may be used for a brief Liturgy of the Word. Other readings may be chosen, for example: Mark 5:21–23, 35–43, Jesus raises the daughter of Jairus and gives her back to her parents; Mark 9:14–27, Jesus cures a boy and gives him back to his father; Luke 7:11–15, Jesus raises a young man, the only son of his mother, and gives him back to her; John 4:46–53, Jesus gives his second sign by healing an official's son. In addition, other stories concerning the Lord's healing ministry may be found suitable, especially if told with the simplicity and clarity of one of the children's versions of Scripture.

A   *Mark 9:33–37*

Jesus proposes the child as the ideal of those who would enter the kingdom.

B   *Mark 10:13–16*

Jesus welcomes the children and lays hands on them.

RESPONSE

67   After the reading of the word of God, time may be set apart for silent reflection if the child is capable of this form of prayer. The minister should also explain the meaning of the reading to those present, adapting it to their circumstances.

The minister may then help the child and the family to respond to the word of God. The following short responsory may be used:

Jesus, come to me.

—Jesus, come to me.

Jesus, put your hand on me.

—Jesus, put your hand on me.

Jesus, bless me.

—Jesus, bless me.

The Lord's Prayer

68 *The minister introduces the Lord's Prayer in these or similar words:*

Let us pray to the Father using those words which Jesus himself used:

All say:

Our Father . . .

Concluding Prayer

69 *The minister says a concluding prayer. One of the following may be used.*

A

God of love,
ever caring,
ever strong,
stand by us in our time of need.

Watch over your child **N.** who is sick,
look after him/her in every danger,
and grant him/her your healing and peace.

We ask this in the name of Jesus the Lord.

R. *Amen.*

B

Father,
in your love
you gave us Jesus
to help us rise triumphant over grief and pain.

Look on your child **N.** who is sick
and see in his/her sufferings those of your Son.

Grant **N.** a share in the strength you granted your Son
that he/she too may be a sign
of your goodness, kindness, and loving care.

We ask this in the name of Jesus the Lord.
R. *Amen.*

BLESSING

*70   The minister makes a Sign of the Cross on the child's forehead,
saying one of the following:*

A

N., when you were baptized,
you were marked with the Cross of Jesus.
I (we) make this cross **✚** on your forehead
and ask the Lord to bless you,
and restore you to health.

R. *Amen.*

B

All praise and glory is yours, heavenly God,
for you have called us to serve you in love.
Have mercy on us and listen to our prayer
as we ask you to help **N.**

Bless ✚ your beloved child,
and restore him/her to health
in the name of Jesus the Lord.

R. Amen.

Each one present may in turn trace the Sign of the Cross on the child's forehead, in silence.

A minister who is not a Priest or Deacon invokes God's blessing and makes the Sign of the Cross on himself or herself, while saying.

May the Lord bless us,
protect us from all evil,
and bring us to everlasting life.

R. Amen.

Communion of the Sick

INTRODUCTION

Whoever eats this bread will live for ever.

71   This chapter contains two rites: one for use when Communion can be celebrated in the context of a Liturgy of the Word; the other, a brief Communion rite for use in more restrictive circumstances, such as in hospitals.

72   Priests with pastoral responsibilities should see to it that the sick or aged, even though not seriously ill or in danger of death, are given every opportunity to receive the Eucharist frequently, even daily, especially during Easter Time. They may receive Communion at any hour. Those who care for the sick may receive Communion with them, in accord with the usual norms. To provide frequent Communion for the sick, it may be necessary to ensure that the community has a sufficient number of Extraordinary Ministers of Holy Communion. The minister should wear attire appropriate to this ministry.

The sick person and others may help to plan the celebration, for example, by choosing the prayers and readings. Those making these choices should keep in mind the condition of the sick person. The readings should help those present to reach a deeper understanding of the mystery of human suffering in relation to the Paschal Mystery of Christ.

73   The faithful who are ill are deprived of their rightful and accustomed place in the Eucharistic community. In bringing Communion to them the Extraordinary Minister of Holy Communion represents Christ and manifests faith and charity on behalf of the whole community toward those who cannot be present at the Eucharist. For the sick the reception of Communion is not only a privilege but also a sign of support and concern shown by the Christian community for its members who are ill.

The links between the community's Eucharistic celebration, especially on the Lord's Day, and the Communion of the sick are intimate and manifold. Besides remembering the sick in the Universal Prayer at Mass, those present should be reminded occasionally of the significance of Communion in the lives of those who are ill: union with Christ in his struggle with evil, his prayer for the world, and his love for the Father, and union with the community from which they are separated.

The obligation to visit and comfort those who cannot take part in the Eucharistic assembly may be clearly demonstrated by taking Communion to them from the community's Eucharistic celebration. This symbol of unity between the community and its sick members has the deepest significance on the Lord's Day, the special day of the Eucharistic assembly.

74 When the Eucharist is brought to the sick, it should be carried in a pyx or small closed container. Those who are with the sick should be asked to prepare a table covered with a linen cloth upon which the Blessed Sacrament will be placed. Lighted candles are prepared and, where it is customary, a vessel of holy water. Care should be taken to make the occasion special and joyful.

Sick people who are unable to receive Communion under the form of bread may receive it under the form of wine alone. If the wine is consecrated at a Mass not celebrated in the presence of the sick person, the Blood of the Lord is kept in a properly covered vessel and is placed in the tabernacle after Communion. The Precious Blood should be carried to the sick in a vessel which is closed in such a way as to eliminate all danger of spilling. If some of the Precious Blood remains, it should be consumed by the minister, who should also see to it that the vessel is properly purified afterward by a Priest or Deacon.

75   If the sick wish to celebrate the Sacrament of Penance, it is preferable that the Priest make himself available for this during a previous visit.

76   If it is necessary to celebrate the Sacrament of Penance during the rite of Communion, it takes the place of the Penitential Act.

COMMUNION IN ORDINARY CIRCUMSTANCES

77   If possible, provision should be made to celebrate Mass in the homes of the sick, with their families and friends gathered around them. The Ordinary determines the conditions and requirements for such celebrations.

COMMUNION IN A HOSPITAL OR INSTITUTION

78   There will be situations, particularly in large institutions with many communicants, when the minister should consider alternative means so that the rite of Communion of the sick is not diminished to the absolute minimum. In such cases the following alternatives should be considered: (a) where possible, the residents or patients may be gathered in groups in one or more areas; (b) additional ministers of Communion may assist.
     When it is not possible to celebrate the full rite, the rite for Communion in a hospital or institution may be used. If it is convenient, however, the minister may add elements from the rite for ordinary circumstances, for example, a Scripture reading.

79   The rite begins with the recitation of the Eucharistic antiphon in the church, the hospital chapel, or the first room visited. Then the minister gives Communion to the sick in their individual rooms.

80   The concluding prayer may be said in the church, the hospital chapel, or the last room visited. No blessing is given.

Communion in Ordinary Circumstances

Introductory Rites

Greeting

81   The minister greets the sick person and the others present. One of the following may be used:

A

Peace be with this house and with all who live here.

B

The peace of the Lord be with you.

C

The grace of our Lord Jesus Christ
and the love of God
and the communion of the Holy Spirit be with you all.

D

Grace to you and peace from God our Father
and the Lord Jesus Christ.

If the minister is not a Priest or Deacon, he or she adds to the greeting:
Blessed be God for ever, *to which all respond:*

Blessed be God for ever.

The minister then places the Blessed Sacrament on the table and all join in adoration.

PENITENTIAL ACT

83   The minister invites the sick person and all present to join in the Penitential Act, using these words:

My brothers and sisters, to prepare ourselves for this celebration, let us call to mind our sins.

After a brief period of silence, the Penitential Act continues, using one of the following:

A

All say:

I confess to almighty God,
and to you, my brothers and sisters,
that I have greatly sinned,
in my thoughts and in my words,
in what I have done, and in what I have failed to do;

And, striking their breast, they say:

through my fault, through my fault,
through my most grievous fault;

Then they continue:

therefore I ask blessed Mary ever-virgin,
all the Angels and Saints,
and you, my brothers and sisters,
to pray for me to the Lord our God.

B

Have mercy on us, O Lord.
R. For we have sinned against you.
Show us, O Lord, your mercy.

R. *And grant us your salvation.*

C

By your Paschal Mystery
   you have won for us salvation:
Lord, have mercy.

R. *Lord, have mercy.*

You renew among us now
   the wonders of your Passion:
Christ, have mercy.

R. *Christ, have mercy.*

When we receive your Body
you share with us your Paschal sacrifice:
Lord, have mercy.

R. *Lord, have mercy.*

The minister concludes the Penitential Act with the following:

May almighty God have mercy on us,
forgive us our sins,
and bring us to everlasting life.

R. *Amen.*

LITURGY OF THE WORD

Reading

84   The word of God is proclaimed by one of those present or by the minister. An appropriate reading from Part III or one of the following readings may be used:

A John 6:51

B John 6:54–58

C John 14:6

D John 15:5

E 1 John 4:16

Response

85   A brief period of silence may be observed after the reading of the word of God.

The minister may then give a brief explanation of the reading, applying it to the needs of the sick person and those who are looking after him or her.

UNIVERSAL PRAYER

86   The Universal Prayer (Prayer of the Faithful) may be said. With a brief introduction the minister invites all those present to pray. After the intentions the minister says the concluding prayer. It is desirable that the intentions be announced by someone other than the minister.

LITURGY OF HOLY COMMUNION

The Lord's Prayer

87   The minister introduces the Lord's Prayer in these or similar words:

A

Now let us pray as Christ the Lord has taught us:

B

And now let us pray with confidence as Christ our Lord commanded:

All say:

Our Father . . .

Communion

88   The minister shows the Eucharistic Bread to those present, saying:

Behold the Lamb of God,
behold him who takes away the sins of the world.
Blessed are those called to the supper of the Lamb.

The sick person and all who are to receive Communion say:

Lord, I am not worthy
that you should enter under my roof,
but only say the word
and my soul shall be healed.

The minister goes to the sick person and, showing the Blessed Sacrament, says:

The Body of Christ.

The sick person answers: Amen, *and receives Communion.*

Then if the Blood of Christ is to be given, the minister says:

The Blood of Christ.

The sick person answers: Amen, *and receives Communion. Others present who wish to receive Communion then do so in the usual way.*

Silent Prayer

89   Then a period of silence may be observed.

Prayer after Communion

90   The minister says a concluding prayer. One of the following may be used:

Let us pray.

Pause for silent prayer, if this has not preceded.

A

All-powerful and ever-living God,
may the Body and Blood of Christ your Son
be for our brother/sister **N.**
a lasting remedy for body and soul.
Through Christ our Lord.
R. *Amen.*

B

O God, who have accomplished the work of
        human redemption
through the Paschal Mystery of your Only Begotten Son,
graciously grant that we, who confidently proclaim,
under sacramental signs, the Death and Resurrection
        of Christ,
may experience continued increase of your saving grace.
Through Christ our Lord.
R. *Amen.*

C

O God, who willed that we be partakers
in the one Bread and the one Chalice,
grant us, we pray, so to live
that, made one in Christ,
we may joyfully bear fruit
for the salvation of the world.
Through Christ our Lord.

R. *Amen.*

D

Nourished by this sacred gift, O Lord,
we give you thanks and beseech your mercy,
that, by the pouring forth of your Spirit,
the grace of integrity may endure
in those your heavenly power has entered.
Through Christ our Lord.

R. *Amen.*

Concluding Rite

Blessing

91   A minister who is not a Priest or Deacon invokes God's blessing and makes the Sign of the Cross on himself or herself, while saying:

A

May the Lord bless us,
protect us from all evil,
and bring us to everlasting life.

R. *Amen.*

B

May the almighty and merciful God bless and protect us,
the Father, and the Son, and the Holy Spirit.

R. *Amen.*

Communion in a Hospital
or Institution

Introductory Rite

Antiphon

*92   The rite may begin in the church, the hospital chapel, or the first
room, where the minister says one of the following antiphons:*

A

How holy this feast
in which Christ is our food:
his passion is recalled;
grace fills our hearts;
and we receive a pledge of the glory to come.

B

How gracious you are, Lord:
your gift of bread from heaven
reveals a Father's love and brings us perfect joy.
You fill the hungry with good things
and send the rich away empty.

C

I am the living bread
come down from heaven.
If you eat this bread
you will live for ever.
The bread I will give is my flesh
for the life of the world.

If it is customary, the minister may be accompanied by a person carrying a candle.

Liturgy of Holy Communion

Greeting

93   *On entering each room, the minister may use one of the following greetings:*

A

The peace of the Lord be with you.

B

The grace of our Lord Jesus Christ
and the love of God
and the communion of the Holy Spirit be with you all.

If the minister is not a Priest or Deacon, he or she adds to the greeting:
Blessed be God for ever, *to which all respond:*

Blessed be God for ever.

The minister then places the Blessed Sacrament on the table, and all join in adoration.

If there is time and it seems desirable, the minister may proclaim a Scripture reading from those found in no. 84 or those appearing in Part III.

The Lord's Prayer

94   *When circumstances permit (for example, when there are not many rooms to visit), the minister is encouraged to lead the sick in the Lord's Prayer. The minister introduces the Lord's Prayer in these or similar words:*

A

Now let us pray as Christ the Lord has taught us:

B

And now let us pray with confidence as Christ our
Lord commanded:

All say:

Our Father . . .

Communion

95   *The minister shows the Eucharistic Bread to those present, saying:*

Behold the Lamb of God,
behold him who takes away the sins of the world.
Blessed are those called to the supper of the Lamb.

The sick person and all who are to receive Communion say:

Lord, I am not worthy
that you should enter under my roof,
but only say the word
and my soul shall be healed.

The minister goes to the sick person and, showing the Blessed Sacrament, says:
The Body of Christ.

The sick person answers: Amen, *and receives Communion.*

Then if the Blood of Christ is to be given, the minister says:
The Blood of Christ.

The sick person answers: Amen, *and receives Communion.*

Others present who wish to receive Communion then do so in the usual way.

Concluding Rite

Concluding Pryer

96   The concluding prayer may be said either in the last room visited, in the church, or chapel. One of the following may be used:

Let us pray.

Pause for silent prayer, if this has not preceded.

A

All-powerful and ever-living God,
may the Body and Blood of Christ your Son
be for our brothers and sisters
a lasting remedy for body and soul.
Through Christ our Lord.

R. *Amen.*

B

O God, who have accomplished the work of human
        redemption
through the Paschal Mystery of your Only Begotten Son,
graciously grant that we, who confidently proclaim,
under sacramental signs, the Death and Resurrection
        of Christ,
may experience continued increase of your saving grace.
Through Christ our Lord.

R. *Amen.*

C

O God, who have willed that we be partakers
in the one Bread and the one Chalice,
grant us, we pray, so to live
that, made one in Christ,
we may joyfully bear fruit
for the salvation of the world.
Through Christ our Lord.

R. *Amen.*

D

Nourished by this sacred gift, O Lord,
we give you thanks and beseech your mercy,
that, by the pouring forth of your Spirit,
the grace of integrity may endure
in those your heavenly power has entered.
Through Christ our Lord.

R. *Amen.*

The blessing is omitted.

Pastoral Care of
the Dying

INTRODUCTION

*When we were baptized in Christ Jesus we were baptized into his death . . .
so that as Christ was raised from the dead by the Father's glory, we too
might live a new life.*

161   The rites in Part II of *Pastoral Care of the Sick: Rites of Anointing
and Viaticum* are used by the Church to comfort and strengthen a dying
Christian in the passage from this life. The ministry to the dying places
emphasis on trust in the Lord's promise of eternal life rather than on
the struggle against illness which is characteristic of the pastoral care
of the sick.

The first three chapters of Part II provide for those situations
in which time is not a pressing concern and the rites can be celebrated
fully and properly. These are to be clearly distinguished from the rites
contained in Chapter Eight, "Rites for Exceptional Circumstances,"
which provide for the emergency situations sometimes encountered in
the ministry to the dying.

162   Priests with pastoral responsibilities are to direct the efforts of
the family and friends as well as other ministers of the local Church in
the care of the dying. They should ensure that all are familiar with the
rites provided here.

The words "Priest," "Deacon," and "minister" are used advisedly.
Only in those rites which must be celebrated by a Priest is the word
"Priest" used in the rubrics (that is, the Sacrament of Penance, the
Sacrament of the Anointing of the Sick, the celebration of Viaticum
within Mass). Whenever it is clear that, in the absence of a Priest, a
Deacon may preside at a particular rite, the words "Priest or Deacon,"
are used in the rubrics. Whenever another minister is permitted to
celebrate a rite in the absence of a Priest or Deacon, the word "minister"

is used in the rubrics, even though in many cases the rite will be celebrated by a Priest or Deacon.

163   The Christian community has a continuing responsibility to pray for and with the person who is dying. Through its sacramental ministry to the dying the community helps Christians to embrace death in mysterious union with the crucified and risen Lord, who awaits them in the fullness of life.

CELEBRATION OF VIATICUM

164   A rite for Viaticum within Mass and another for Viaticum outside Mass are provided. If possible, and with the permission of the Ordinary, Viaticum should take place within the full Eucharistic celebration, with the family, friends, and other members of the Christian community taking part. The rite for Viaticum outside Mass is used when the full Eucharistic celebration cannot take place. Again, if it is possible, others should take part.

COMMENDATION OF THE DYING

165   The second chapter of Part II contains a collection of prayers for the spiritual comfort of the Christian who is close to death. These prayers are traditionally called the commendation of the dying to God and are to be used according to the circumstances of each case.

PRAYERS FOR THE DEAD

166   A chapter has also been provided to assist a minister who has been called to attend a person who is already dead. A Priest is not to administer the Sacrament of Anointing. Instead, he should pray for the dead person, using prayers such as those which appear in this chapter. He may find it necessary to explain to the family of the person who is dead that sacraments are celebrated for the living, not for the dead, and that the dead are effectively helped by the prayers of the living.

Rites for Exceptional Circumstances

167   Chapter Eight, "Rites for Exceptional Circumstances," contains rites which should be celebrated with a person who has suddenly been placed in proximate or immediate danger of death. They are for emergency circumstances and should be used only when such pressing conditions exist.

Care of a Dying Child

168   In its ministry to the dying the Church must also respond to the difficult circumstances of a dying child. Although no specific rites appear in Part II for the care of a dying child, these notes are provided to help bring into focus the various aspects of this ministry.

169   When parents learn that their child is dying, they are often bewildered and hurt. In their love for their son or daughter, they may be beset by temptations and doubts and find themselves asking: Why is God taking this child from us? How have we sinned or failed that God would punish us in this way? Why is this innocent child being hurt?

Under these trying circumstances, much of the Church's ministry will be directed to the parents and family. While pain and suffering in an innocent child are difficult for others to bear, the Church helps the parents and family to accept what God has allowed to happen. It should be understood by all beforehand that this process of acceptance will probably extend beyond the death of the child. The concern of the Christian community should continue as long as necessary.

Concern for the child must be equal to that for the family. Those who deal with dying children observe that their faith matures rapidly. Though young children often seem to accept death more easily than adults, they will often experience a surprisingly mature anguish because of the pain which they see in their families.

170   At such a time, it is important for members of the Christian community to come to the support of the child and the family by prayer, visits, and other forms of assistance. Those who have lost children of their own have a ministry of consolation and support to the family. Hospital personnel (doctors, nurses, aides) should also be prepared to exercise a special role with the child as caring adults. Priests and Deacons bear particular responsibility for overseeing all these elements of the Church's pastoral ministry. The minister should invite members of the community to use their individual gifts in this work of communal care and concern.

171   By conversation and brief services of readings and prayers, the minister may help the parents and family to see that their child is being called ahead of them to enter the kingdom and joy of the Lord. The period when the child is dying can become a special time of renewal and prayer for the family and close friends. The minister should help them to see that the child's sufferings are united to those of Jesus for the salvation of the whole world.

172   If it is appropriate, the Priest should discuss with the parents the possibility of preparing and celebrating with the child the Sacraments of Initiation (Baptism, Confirmation, Eucharist). The Priest may baptize and confirm the child (see *Rite of Confirmation,* no. 7b). To complete the process of Initiation, the child should also receive first Communion.

According to the circumstances, some of these rites may be celebrated by a Deacon or layperson. So that the child and family may receive full benefit from them, these rites are normally celebrated over a period of time. In this case, the minister should use the usual rites, that is, the *Rite of Baptism for Children,* the *Rite of Confirmation,* and if suitable, the *Rite of Penance.* Similarly, if time allows, the usual rites for Anointing and Viaticum should be celebrated.

173   If sudden illness or an accident has placed an uninitiated child in proximate danger of death, the minister uses "Christian Initiation for the Dying," adapting it for use with a child.

174   For an initiated child or a child lacking only the Sacrament of Confirmation, who is in proximate danger of death, the "Continuous Rite of Penance, Anointing, and Viaticum" may be used and adapted to the understanding of the child. If death is imminent it should be remembered that Viaticum rather than Anointing is the sacrament for the dying.

Celebration of Viaticum

INTRODUCTION

I am going to prepare a place for you; I shall come back and take you with me.

175   This chapter contains a rite for Viaticum within Mass and a rite for Viaticum outside Mass. The celebration of the Eucharist as Viaticum, food for the passage through death to eternal life, is the sacrament proper to the dying Christian. It is the completion and crown of the Christian life on this earth, signifying that the Christian follows the Lord to eternal glory and the banquet of the heavenly kingdom.

The Sacrament of the Anointing of the Sick should be celebrated at the beginning of a serious illness. Viaticum, celebrated when death is close, will then be better understood as the last sacrament of Christian life.

176   Priests and other ministers entrusted with the spiritual care of the sick should do everything they can to ensure that those in proximate danger of death receive the Body and Blood of Christ as Viaticum. At the earliest opportunity, the necessary preparation should be given to the dying person, family, and others who may take part.

177   Whenever it is possible, the dying Christian should be able to receive Viaticum within Mass. In this way he or she shares fully, during the final moments of this life, in the Eucharistic Sacrifice, which proclaims the Lord's own passing through death to life. However, circumstances, such as confinement to a hospital ward or the very emergency which makes death imminent, may frequently make the complete Eucharistic celebration impossible. In this case, the rite for Viaticum outside Mass is appropriate. The minister should wear attire appropriate to this ministry.

178   Because the celebration of Viaticum ordinarily takes place in the limited circumstances of the home, a hospital, or other institution,

the simplifications of the rite for Masses in small gatherings may be appropriate. Depending on the condition of the dying person, every effort should be made to involve him or her, the family, friends, and other members of the local community in the planning and celebration. Appropriate readings, prayers, and songs will help to foster the full participation of all. Because of this concern for participation, the minister should ensure that Viaticum is celebrated while the dying person is still able to take part and respond.

179   A distinctive feature of the celebration of Viaticum, whether within or outside Mass, is the renewal of the baptismal profession of faith by the dying person. This occurs after the Homily and replaces the usual form of the Profession of Faith. Through the baptismal profession at the end of earthly life, the one who is dying uses the language of his or her initial commitment, which is renewed each Easter and on other occasions in the Christian life. In the context of Viaticum, it is a renewal and fulfillment of initiation into the Christian mysteries, Baptism leading to the Eucharist.

180   The rites for Viaticum within and outside Mass may include the sign of peace. The minister and all who are present embrace the dying Christian. In this and in other parts of the celebration the sense of leave-taking need not be concealed or denied, but the joy of Christian hope, which is the comfort and strength of the one near death, should also be evident.

181   As an indication that the reception of the Eucharist by the dying Christian is a pledge of resurrection and food for the passage through death, the special words proper to Viaticum are added: "May the Lord Jesus Christ protect you and lead you to eternal life." The dying person and all who are present may receive Communion under both kinds. The sign of Communion is more complete when received in this manner because it expresses more fully and clearly the nature of the Eucharist as a meal, one which prepares all who take part in it for the heavenly banquet (see the *General Instruction of the Roman Missal,* no. 281).

The minister should choose the manner of giving Communion under both kinds which is suitable in the particular case. If the wine is consecrated at a Mass not celebrated in the presence of the sick person, the Blood of the Lord is kept in a properly covered vessel and is placed in the tabernacle after Communion. The Precious Blood should be carried to the sick person in a vessel which is closed in such a way as to eliminate all danger of spilling. If some of the Precious Blood remains after Communion, it should be consumed by the minister, who should also see to it that the vessel is properly purified afterward by a Priest or Deacon.

The sick who are unable to receive under the form of bread may receive under the form of wine alone. If the wine is consecrated at a Mass not celebrated in the presence of the sick person, the instructions given above are followed.

182   In addition to these elements of the rites which are to be given greater stress, special texts are provided for the Universal Prayer or litany and the final Solemn Blessing.

183   It often happens that a person who has received the Eucharist as Viaticum lingers in a grave condition or at the point of death for a period of days or longer. In these circumstances he or she should be given the opportunity to receive the Eucharist as Viaticum on successive days, frequently if not daily. This may take place during or outside Mass as particular conditions permit. The rite may be simplified according to the condition of the one who is dying.

Viaticum within Mass

184   When Viaticum is received within Mass, the ritual Mass for Viaticum or the Mass of the Holy Eucharist may be celebrated. The priest wears white vestments. The readings may be taken from the *Lectionary for Mass* (second edition, nos. 796–800), unless the dying person and those involved with the Priest in planning the liturgy choose other readings from Scripture.

A ritual Mass is not permitted during the Easter Triduum, on the Solemnities of Christmas, Epiphany, Ascension, Pentecost, Corpus Christi, or on a Solemnity which is a Holyday of Obligation. On these occasions, the texts and readings are taken from the Mass of the day. Although the Mass for Viaticum or the Mass of the Holy Eucharist are also excluded on the Sundays of Advent, Lent, and Easter Time, on Solemnities, Ash Wednesday, and the weekdays of Holy Week, one of the readings may be taken from the biblical texts indicated above. The special form of the final blessing may be used and, at the discretion of the Priest, the Apostolic Pardon may be added.

185 If the dying person wishes to celebrate the Sacrament of Penance, it is preferable that the Priest make himself available for this during a previous visit. If this is not possible, the Sacrament of Penance may be celebrated before Mass begins (see Appendix, p. 372).

VIATICUM OUTSIDE MASS

186 Although Viaticum celebrated in the context of the full Eucharistic celebration is always preferable, when it is not possible the rite for Viaticum outside Mass is appropriate. This rite includes some of the elements of the Mass, especially a brief Liturgy of the Word. Depending on the circumstances and the condition of the dying person, this rite should also be a communal celebration. Every effort should be made to involve the dying person, family, friends, and members of the local community in the planning and celebration. The manner of celebration and the elements of the rite which are used should be accommodated to those present and the nearness of death.

187 If the dying person wishes to celebrate the Sacrament of Penance and this cannot take place during a previous visit, it should be celebrated before the rite of Viaticum begins, especially if others are present. Alternatively, it may be celebrated during the rite of Viaticum, replacing the Penitential Act. At the discretion of the Priest, the Apostolic Pardon may be added after the Penitential Act or after the Sacrament of Penance.

188 An abbreviated Liturgy of the Word, ordinarily consisting of a single biblical reading, gives the minister an opportunity to explain the word of God in relation to Viaticum. The sacrament should be described as the sacred food which strengthens the Christian for the passage through death to life in sure hope of the resurrection.

Viaticum outside Mass

Introductory Rites

Greeting

197   The minister greets the sick person and the others present.
The following may be used:

A

Peace be with this house and with all who live here.

B

The peace of the Lord be with you.

C

The grace of our Lord Jesus Christ
and the love of God
and the communion of the Holy Spirit be with you all.

D

Grace to you and peace from God our Father
and the Lord Jesus Christ.

If the minister is not a Priest or Deacon, he or she adds to the greeting:
Blessed be God for ever, to which all respond:

Blessed be God for ever.

The minister then places the Blessed Sacrament on the table, and all join
in adoration.

Instruction

199   Afterward the minister addresses those present, using the following instruction or one better suited to the sick person's condition:

My brothers and sisters, before our Lord Jesus Christ passed from this world to return to the Father, he left us the sacrament of his Body and Blood. When the hour comes for us to pass from this life and join him, he strengthens us with this food for our journey and comforts us by this pledge of our resurrection.

Penitential Act

200   The minister invites the sick person and all present to join in the Penitential Act, using these words:

My brothers and sisters, to prepare ourselves for this celebration, let us call to mind our sins.

After a brief period of silence, the Penitential Act continues using one of the following prayers.

A   *All say:*

I confess to almighty God,
and to you, my brothers and sisters,
that I have greatly sinned,
in my thoughts and in my words,
in what I have done, and in what I have failed to do;

And, striking thier breast, they say:
through my fault, through my fault,
through my most grievous fault;

Then they continue:

therefore I ask blessed Mary ever-virgin,
all the Angels and Saints,
and you, my brothers and sisters,
to pray for me to the Lord our God.

B

By your Paschal Mystery
  you have won for us salvation:
Lord, have mercy.

R. *Lord, have mercy.*

You renew among us now
  the wonders of your Passion:
Christ, have mercy.

R. *Christ, have mercy.*

When we receive your Body,
you share with us your Paschal sacrifice:
Lord, have mercy.

R. *Lord, have mercy.*

The minister concludes the Penitential Act with the following:
May almighty God have mercy us,
forgive us our sins,
and bring us to everlasting life.

R. *Amen.*

Liturgy of the Word

Reading

202   The word of God is proclaimed by one of those present or by the minister. An appropriate reading from Part III or one of the following may be used:

A John 6:54–55

B John 14:23

C John 15:4

D 1 Corinthians 11:26

Homily

203   Depending on circumstances, the minister may then give a brief explanation of the reading.

Baptismal Profession of Faith

204   It is desirable that the sick person renew his or her baptismal profession of faith before receiving Viaticum. The minister gives a brief introduction and then asks the following questions:

N., do you believe in God,
the Father almighty,
Creator of heaven and earth?

R. *I do.*

Do you believe in Jesus Christ, his only Son, our Lord,
who was born of the Virgin Mary,
suffered death and was buried,
rose again from the dead
and is seated at the right hand of the Father?

R. *I do.*

Do you believe in the Holy Spirit,
the holy Catholic Church,
the communion of saints,
the forgiveness of sins,
the resurrection of the body,
and life everlasting?

R. I do.

Litany

*205   The minister may adapt or shorten the litany according to the
condition of the sick person. The litany may be omitted if the sick person
has made the Profession of Faith and appears to be tiring.*

My brothers and sisters, with one heart let us call on our
Savior Jesus Christ.

You loved us to the very end and gave yourself over to death
in order to give us life. For our brother/sister, Lord, we pray:

R. Lord, hear our prayer.

You said to us: "All who eat my flesh and drink my blood will
live for ever." For our brother/sister, Lord, we pray:

R. Lord, hear our prayer.

You invite us to join in the banquet where pain and sorrow,
sadness and separation will be no more. For our brother/
sister, Lord, we pray:

R. Lord, hear our prayer.

LITURGY OF VIATICUM

The Lord's Prayer

206   The minister introduces the Lord's Prayer in these words:

A

Now let us offer together the prayer our Lord Jesus Christ taught us:

B

And now let us pray with confidence as Christ our Lord commanded:

All say:

Our Father . . .

Communion as Viaticum

207   The sick person and all present may receive Communion under both kinds. When the minister gives Communion to the sick person, the form for Viaticum is used.

The minister shows the Eucharistic Bread to those present, saying:

Behold the Lamb of God,
behold him who takes away the sins of the world.
Blessed are those called to the supper of the Lamb.

The sick person and all who are to receive Communion say:

Lord, I am not worthy
that you should enter under my roof,
but only say the word
and my soul shall be healed.

The minister goes to the sick person and, showing the Blessed Sacrament, says:

The Body of Christ.

The sick person answers: Amen.

Then if the Blood of Christ is to be given, the minister says:

The Blood of Christ.

The sick person answers: Amen.

Immediately, or after giving Communion to the sick person, the minister adds:

May the Lord Jesus Christ protect you
and lead you to eternal life.

R. *Amen.*

Others present who wish to receive Communion then do so in the usual way.

After the conclusion of the rite, the minister cleanses the vessel as usual.

Silent Prayer

208   *Then a period of silence may be observed.*

Prayer after Communion

209   *The minister says the concluding prayer.*

Let us pray.

Pause for silent prayer, if this has not preceded.

A

O God, whose Son is for us the way, the truth and the life,
look lovingly upon your servant **N.**
and grant that, trusting in your promises
and strengthened by the Body of your Son,
he (she) may journey in peace to your Kingdom.
Through Christ our Lord.

R. *Amen.*

B

O Lord, eternal health and salvation
of those who believe in you,
grant, we pray, that your servant **N.,**
renewed by heavenly food and drink,
may safely reach your Kingdom of light and life.
Through Christ our Lord.

R. *Amen.*

C

All-powerful and ever-living God,
may the Body and Blood of Christ your Son
be for our brother/sister **N.**
a lasting remedy for body and soul.

Through Christ our Lord.
R. *Amen.*

Concluding Rites

Blessing

210   A minister who is not a Priest or Deacon invokes God's blessing and makes the Sign of the Cross on himself or herself, while saying:

A

May the Lord bless us,
protect us from all evil,
and bring us to everlasting life.

R. *Amen.*

B

May the almighty and merciful God bless and protect us,
the Father, and the Son, and the Holy Spirit.

R. *Amen.*

Sign of Peace

211   The minister and the others present may then give the sick person the sign of peace.

Commendation
of the Dying

INTRODUCTION

Into your hands, Lord, I commend my spirit.

212   In Viaticum the dying person is united with Christ in his passage out of this world to the Father. Through the prayers for the commendation of the dying contained in this chapter, the Church helps to sustain this union until it is brought to fulfillment after death.

213   Christians have the responsibility of expressing their union in Christ by joining the dying person in prayer for God's mercy and for confidence in Christ. In particular, the presence of a Priest or Deacon shows more clearly that the Christian dies in the communion of the Church. He should assist the dying person and those present in the recitation of the prayers of commendation and, following death, he should lead those present in the prayer after death. If the Priest or Deacon is unable to be present because of other serious pastoral obligations, other members of the community should be prepared to assist with these prayers and should have the texts readily available to them.

214   The minister may choose texts from among the prayers, litanies, aspirations, psalms, and readings provided in this chapter, or others may be added. In the selection of these texts the minister should keep in mind the condition and piety of both the dying person and the members of the family who are present. The prayers are best said in a slow, quiet voice, alternating with periods of silence. If possible, the minister says one or more of the brief prayer formulas with the dying person. These may be softly repeated two or three times.

215   These texts are intended to help the dying person, if still conscious, to face the natural human anxiety about death by imitating

Christ in his patient suffering and dying. The Christian will be helped to surmount his or her fear in the hope of heavenly life and resurrection through the power of Christ, who destroyed the power of death by his own dying.

Even if the dying person is not conscious, those who are present will draw consolation from these prayers and come to a better understanding of the paschal character of Christian death. This may be visibly expressed by making the Sign of the Cross on the forehead of the dying person, who was first signed with the cross at Baptism.

216   Immediately after death has occurred, all may kneel while one of those present leads the prayers given on nos. 221–222.

SHORT TEXTS

217   One or more of the following short texts may be recited with the dying person. If necessary, they may be softly repeated two or three times.

Romans 8:35
Who can separate us from the love of Christ?

Romans 14:8
Whether we live or die, we are the Lord's.

2 Corinthians 5:1
We have an everlasting home in heaven.

1 Thessalonians 4:17
We shall be with the Lord for ever.

1 John 3:2
We shall see God as he really is.

1 John 3:14
We have passed from death to life
because we love each other.

Psalm 25:1
To you, Lord, I lift up my soul.

Psalm 27:1
The Lord is my light and my salvation.

Psalm 27:13
I believe that I shall see the goodness of the Lord
in the land of the living.

Psalm 42:3
My soul thirsts for the living God.

Psalm 23:4
Though I walk in the shadow of death,
I will fear no evil, for you are with me.

Matthew 25:34
Come, blessed of my Father,
says the Lord Jesus,
and take possession of the kingdom
prepared for you.

Luke 23:43
The Lord Jesus says,
today you will be with me in paradise.

John 14:2
In my Father's home
there are many dwelling places,
says the Lord Jesus.

John 14:2–3
The Lord Jesus says,
I go to prepare a place for you,
and I will come again to take you to myself.

John 17:24
I desire that where I am,
they also may be with me,
says the Lord Jesus.

John 6:40
Everyone who believes in the Son
has eternal life.

Psalm 31:6a
Into your hands, Lord,
I commend my spirit.

Acts 7:59
Lord Jesus, receive my spirit.

Holy Mary, pray for me.

Saint Joseph, pray for me.

Jesus, Mary, and Joseph,
assist me in my last agony.

Reading

218   The word of God is proclaimed by one of those present or by the minister. Selections from Part III or from the following readings may be used:

A. Job 19:23–27
Job's act of faith is a model for our own; God is the God of the living.

B. Psalm 23

C. Psalm 25

D. Psalm 91

E. Psalm 121

F. 1 John 4:16

G. Revelation 21:1–5a, 6–7
God our Father is the God of newness of life; it is his desire that we should come to share his life with him.

H. Matthew 25:1–13
Jesus bid us be prepared for our ultimate destiny, which is eternal life.

I. Luke 22:39–46
Jesus is alive to our pain and sorrow, because faithfulness to his Father's will cost him life itself.

J. Luke 23:44–49
Jesus' death is witnessed by his friends.

K. *Luke 24:1–8*
Jesus is alive; he gives us eternal life with the Father.

L. *John 6:37–40*
Jesus will raise his own from death and give them eternal life.

M. *John 14:1–6, 23, 27*
The love of Jesus can raise us up from the sorrow of death to the joy of eternal life.

Litany of the Saints

219   When the condition of the dying person calls for the use of brief forms of prayer, those who are present are encouraged to pray the Litany of the Saints—or at least some of its invocations—for him or her. Special mention may be made of the Patron Saints of the dying person, of the family, and of the parish. The Litany may be said or sung in the usual way. Other customary prayers may also be used.

A

Lord, have mercy . . . . *Lord, have mercy*
Christ, have mercy . . . . *Christ, have mercy*
Lord, have mercy . . . . *Lord, have mercy*

Holy Mary, Mother of God . . . . *pray for him/her*
Holy Angels of God . . . . *pray for him/her*
Abraham, our father in faith. . . . . *pray for him/her*
David, leader of God's people . . . . *pray for him/her*
All holy patriarchs and prophets . . . . *pray for him/her*

Saint John the Baptist. . . . . *pray for him/her*
Saint Joseph. . . . . *pray for him/her*
Saint Peter and Saint Paul . . . . *pray for him/her*
Saint Andrew . . . . *pray for him/her*
Saint John . . . . *pray for him/her*
Saint Mary Magdalene. . . . . *pray for him/her*

Saint Stephen. . . . . *pray for him/her*
Saint Ignatius . . . . *pray for him/her*
Saint Lawrence . . . . *pray for him/her*
Saint Perpetua and Saint Felicity . . . . *pray for him/her*
Saint Agnes . . . . *pray for him/her*
Saint Gregory . . . .*pray for him/her*
Saint Augustine . . . . *pray for him/her*
Saint Athanasius. . . . . *pray for him/her*
Saint Basil . . . . *pray for him/her*
Saint Martin . . . . *pray for him/her*
Saint Benedict. . . . . *pray for him/her*
Saint Francis and Saint Dominic . . . . *pray for him/her*
Saint Francis Xavier . . . . *pray for him/her*
Saint John Vianney . . . . *pray for him/her*
Saint Catherine. . . . . *pray for him/her*
Saint Teresa . . . . *pray for him/her*

Other Saints may be included here.

All holy men and women. . . . . *pray for him/her*

Lord, be merciful . . . . *Lord, save your people*
From all evil . . . . *Lord, save your people*
From every sin . . . . *Lord, save your people*
From Satan's power . . . . *Lord, save your people*
At the moment of death. . . . . *Lord, save your people*
From everlasting death . . . . *Lord, save your people*
On the day of judgment. . . . . *Lord, save your people*
By your coming as man . . . . *Lord, save your people*
By your suffering and Cross . . . . *Lord, save your people*
By your Death
        and rising to new life . . . . *Lord, save your people*

By your return in glory
    to the Father .... *Lord, save your people*
By your gift
    of the Holy Spirit .... *Lord, save your people*
By your coming again
    in glory.................... *Lord, save your people*
Be merciful to us sinners .... *Lord, hear our prayer*
Bring **N.** to eternal life,
    first promised to
    him/her in Baptism .... *Lord, hear our prayer*
Raise **N.** on the last day,
    for he/she has eaten
    the Bread of life............... *Lord, hear our prayer*
Let **N.** share in your glory,
    for he/she has shared
    in your suffering
    and Death .... *Lord, hear our prayer*
Jesus, Son of the living God........... *Lord, hear our prayer*
Christ, hear us........................... *Christ, hear us*
Lord Jesus, hear our prayer .... *Lord, hear our prayer*

B

A brief form of the Litany may be prayed. Other Saints may be added, including the Patron Saints of the dying person, of the family, and of the parish; Saints to whom the dying person may have a special devotion may also be included.

Holy Mary, Mother of God .... *pray for him/her*
Holy Angels of God .... *pray for him/her*
Saint John the Baptist.................... *pray for him/her*
Saint Joseph............................ *pray for him/her*
Saint Peter and Saint Paul .... *pray for him/her*

Other Saints may be included here.

All holy men and women. . . . . *pray for him/her*

Prayer of Commendation

220   When the moment of death seems near, some of the following prayers may be said:

A

Go forth, Christian soul, from this world
in the name of God the almighty Father,
who created you,
in the name of Jesus Christ, Son of the living God,
who suffered for you,
in the name of the Holy Spirit,
who was poured out upon you,
go forth, faithful Christian.

May you live in peace this day,
may your home be with God in Zion,
with Mary, the virgin Mother of God,
with Joseph, and all the Angels and Saints.

B

I commend you, my dear brother/sister,
to almighty God,
and entrust you to your Creator.
May you return to him
who formed you from the dust of the earth.
May holy Mary, the Angels, and all the Saints
come to meet you as you go forth from this life.

May Christ who was crucified for you
bring you freedom and peace.
May Christ who died for you
admit you into his garden of paradise.
May Christ, the true Shepherd,
acknowledge you as one of his flock.
May he forgive all your sins,
and set you among those he has chosen.
May you see your Redeemer face to face,
and enjoy the vision of God for ever.

R. *Amen.*

C

Welcome your servant, Lord, into the place of salvation which because of your mercy he/she rightly hoped for.

R. *Amen,* or **R.** *Lord, save your people.*

Deliver your servant, Lord, from every distress.

R. *Amen,* or **R.** *Lord, save your people.*

Deliver your servant, Lord, as you delivered Noah
from the flood.

R. *Amen,* or **R.** *Lord, save your people.*

Deliver your servant, Lord, as you delivered Abraham from
Ur of the Chaldees.

R. *Amen,* or **R.** *Lord, save your people.*

Deliver your servant, Lord, as you delivered Moses
from the hand of the Pharaoh.

R. *Amen,* or **R.** *Lord, save your people.*

Deliver your servant, Lord, as you delivered Daniel
from the den of lions.

R. *Amen,* or **R.** *Lord, save your people.*

Deliver your servant, Lord, as you delivered the three young
men from the fiery furnace.

R. *Amen,* or **R.** *Lord, save your people.*

Deliver your servant, Lord, as you delivered Susanna
from her false accusers.

R. *Amen,* or **R.** *Lord, save your people.*

Deliver your servant, Lord, as you delivered David
from the attacks of Saul and Goliath.

R. *Amen,* or **R.** *Lord, save your people.*

Deliver your servant, Lord, as you delivered Peter and Paul
from prison.

R. *Amen,* or **R.** *Lord, save your people.*

Deliver your servant, Lord, through Jesus our Savior,
who suffered death for us and gave us eternal life.

R. *Amen,* or **R.** *Lord, save your people.*

D

Lord Jesus Christ, Savior of the world,
we pray for your servant **N.**,
and commend him/her to your mercy.
For his/her sake you came down from heaven;
receive him/her now into the joy of your kingdom.

For though he/she has sinned,
he/she has not denied the Father, the Son, and the Holy Spirit,
but has believed in God
and has worshipped his/her Creator.

R. *Amen.*

E   *The following antiphon may be said or sung:*

Hail, holy Queen, Mother of mercy,
hail, our life, our sweetness, and our hope.
To you we cry, the children of Eve;
to you we send up our sighs,
mourning and weeping in this land of exile.
Turn, then, most gracious advocate,
your eyes of mercy toward us;
lead us home at last
and show us the blessed fruit of your womb, Jesus:
O clement, O loving, O sweet Virgin Mary.

Prayer after Death

221   When death has occurred, one or more of the following prayers may be said:

A

Saints of God, come to his/her aid!
Come to meet him/her, Angels of the Lord!

R. *Receive his/her soul and present him/her to God the Most High.*

May Christ, who called you, take you to himself;
may Angels lead you to Abraham's side.

R. *Receive his/her soul and present him/her to God the Most High.*

Give him/her eternal rest, O Lord,
and may your light shine on him/her for ever.

R. *Receive his/her soul and present him/her to God the Most High.*

The following prayer is added:

Let us pray.

All-powerful and merciful God,
we commend to you **N.**, your servant.
In your mercy and love,
blot out the sins he/she has committed
    through human weakness.
In this world he/she has died:
let him/her live with you for ever.
Through Christ our Lord.

R. *Amen.*

For the solace of those present the minister may conclude these prayers with a simple blessing or with a symbolic gesture, for example, signing the forehead with the Sign of the Cross.

B   PSALM 130

R. My soul hopes in the Lord.

Out of the depths I cry to you, O LORD;
   LORD, hear my voice!
Let your ears be attentive
   to my voice in supplication. ***R.***

I trust in the LORD,
   my soul trusts in his word.
My soul waits for the LORD
   more than sentinels wait for the dawn. ***R.***

For with the LORD is kindness,
   and with him is plenteous redemption.
And he will redeem Israel
   from all their iniquities. ***R.***

The following prayer is added:

Let us pray.
God of love,
welcome into your presence
your son/daughter **N.**, whom you have
     called from this life.
Release him/her from all his/her sins,
bless him/her with eternal light and peace,
raise him/her up to live for ever with all your Saints
in the glory of the resurrection.

Through Christ our Lord.
R. *Amen.*

C   PSALM 23

R. *Lord, remember me in your kingdom.*

The LORD is my shepherd; I shall not want.
     In verdant pastures he gives me repose;
Beside restful waters he leads me;
     he refreshes my soul. **R.**

He guides me in right paths
     for his name's sake.
Even though I walk in the dark valley
     I fear no evil; for you are at my side
With your rod and your staff
     that give me courage. **R.**

You spread the table before me
    in the sight of my foes;
You anoint my head with oil;
    my cup overflows. **R.**

Only goodness and kindness follow me
    all the days of my life;
And I shall dwell in the house of the LORD
    for years to come. **R.**

The following prayer is added:

Let us pray.
God of mercy,
hear our prayers and be merciful
to your son/daughter **N.**,
    whom you have called from this life.
Welcome him/her into the company of your Saints,
in the kingdom of light and peace.

Through Christ our Lord.

R. *Amen.*

D

Almighty and eternal God,
hear our prayers for your son/daughter **N.**,
whom you have called from this life to yourself.
Grant him/her light, happiness, and peace.
Let him/her pass in safety through the gates
of death,
and live for ever with all your Saints
in the light you promised to Abraham
and to all his descendants in faith.

Guard him/her from all harm
and on that great day of resurrection and reward
raise him/her up with all your Saints.
Pardon his/her sins
and give him/her eternal life in your kingdom.

Through Christ our Lord.
R. *Amen.*

E

Loving and merciful God,
we entrust our brother/sister to your mercy.
You loved him/her greatly in this life:
now that he/she is freed from all its cares,
give him/her happiness and peace for ever.

The old order has passed away:
welcome him/her now into paradise
where there will be no more sorrow,
no more weeping or pain,
but only peace and joy

with Jesus, your Son,
and the Holy Spirit
for ever and ever.

R. *Amen.*

F

God of our destiny,
into your hands we commend our brother/sister.
We are confident that with all who have died in Christ
he/she will be raised to life on the last day
and live with Christ for ever.

[We thank you for all the blessings
you gave him/her in this life
to show your fatherly care for all of us
and the fellowship which is ours with the Saints in Jesus Christ.]

Lord, hear our prayer:
welcome our brother/sister to paradise
and help us to comfort each other
with the assurance of our faith
until we all meet in Christ
to be with you and with our brother/sister for ever.

Through Christ our Lord.
R. *Amen.*

Prayer for the Family and Friends

222   The following prayer may be said:

Let us pray.

A   *For the family and friends*

God of all consolation,
in your unending love and mercy for us
you turn the darkness of death
into the dawn of new life.
Show compassion to your people in their sorrow.
[Be our refuge and our strength
to lift us from the darkness of this grief
to the peace and light of your presence.]
Your Son, our Lord Jesus Christ,
by dying for us, conquered death
and by rising again, restored life.
May we then go forward eagerly to meet him,
and after our life on earth
be reunited with our brothers and sisters
where every tear will be wiped away.
Through Christ our Lord.

***R.** Amen.*

B   *For the deceased person and for family and friends*

Lord Jesus, our Redeemer,
you willingly gave yourself up to death
so that all people might be saved
and pass from death into new life.
Listen to our prayers,
look with love on your people
who mourn and pray for their brother/sister **N.**

Lord Jesus, holy and compassionate:
forgive **N.** his/her sins.
By dying you opened the gates of life
for those who believe in you:
do not let our brother/sister be parted from you,
but by your glorious power
give him/her light, joy, and peace in heaven
where you live for ever and ever.
R. *Amen.*

*For the solace of those present the minister may conclude these prayers
with a simple blessing or with a symbolic gesture, for example, signing
the forehead with the Sign of the Cross.*

Prayers for the Dead

INTRODUCTION

I want those you have given me to be with me where I am.

223   This chapter contains prayers for use by a minister who has been called to attend a person who is already dead. A Priest is not to administer the Sacraments of Penance or Anointing. Instead, he should pray for the dead person using these or similar prayers.

224   It may be necessary to explain to the family of the person who is dead that sacraments are celebrated for the living, not for the dead, and that the dead are effectively helped by the prayers of the living.

225   To comfort those present the minister may conclude these prayers with a simple blessing or with a symbolic gesture, for example, making the Sign of the Cross on the forehead. A Priest or Deacon may sprinkle the body with holy water.

Greeting
226   The minister greets those who are present, offering them sympathy and the consolation of faith, using the following or similar words:

A

In this moment of sorrow
the Lord is in our midst
and comforts us with his word:
Blessed are the sorrowful; they shall be consoled.

B

Praised be God, the Father of our Lord Jesus Christ,
the Father of mercies,
and the God of all consolation!
He comforts us in all our afflictions
and thus enables us to comfort those who are in trouble,
with the same consolation
we have received from him.

Prayer

*227   The minister then says one of the following prayers, commending
the person who has just died to God's mercy and goodness:*

Let us pray.

A

Almighty and eternal God,
hear our prayers for your son/daughter **N.**,
whom you have called from this life to yourself.

Grant him/her light, happiness, and peace.
Let him/her pass in safety through the gates of death,
and live for ever with all your Saints
in the light you promised to Abraham
and to all his descendants in faith.

Guard him/her from all harm
and on that great day of resurrection and reward
raise him/her up with all your Saints.
Pardon his/her sins
and give him/her eternal life in your kingdom.

Through Christ our Lord.
R. *Amen.*

B

Loving and merciful God,
we entrust our brother/sister to your mercy.
You loved him/her greatly in this life:
now that he/she is freed from all its cares,
give him/her happiness and peace for ever.

The old order has passed away:
welcome him/her now into paradise
where there will be no more sorrow,
no more weeping or pain,
but only peace and joy
with Jesus, your Son,
and the Holy Spirit
for ever and ever.

R. *Amen.*

Reading

228   The word of God is proclaimed by one of those present or by the minister. One of the following readings may be used:

A Luke 23:44–46
B John 11:3–7, 20–27, 33–36, 41–44

Litany

229   Then one of those present may lead the others in praying a brief form of the Litany of the Saints. (The full form of the Litany of the Saints may be found in no. 219.) Other Saints may be added, including the Patron Saints of the dead person, of the family, and of the parish; Saints to whom the deceased person may have had a special devotion may also be included.

Saints of God, come to his/her aid!
Come to meet him/her, Angels of the Lord!

Holy Mary, Mother of God . . . .*pray for him/her*
Saint Joseph . . . .*pray for him/her*
Saint Peter and Saint Paul . . . .*pray for him/her*

The following prayer is added:

God of mercy,
hear our prayers and be merciful
to your son/daughter **N.**, whom you have called from this life.
Welcome him/her into the company of your Saints,
in the kingdom of light and peace.

Through Christ our Lord.

R. *Amen.*

The Lord's Prayer

230   The minister introduces the Lord's Prayer in these or similar words:

A

With God there is mercy and fullness of redemption; let us pray as Jesus taught us to pray:

B

Let us pray for the coming of the kingdom as Jesus taught us:
All say:

Our Father . . .

Prayer of Commendation

231   *The minister then concludes with the following prayer:*

Lord Jesus, our Redeemer,
you willingly gave yourself up to death
so that all people might be saved
and pass from death into a new life.
Listen to our prayers,
look with love on your people
who mourn and pray for their brother/sister **N.**

Lord Jesus, holy and compassionate:
forgive **N.** his/her sins.
By dying you opened the gates of life
for those who believe in you:
do not let our brother/sister be parted from you,
but by your glorious power
give him/her light, joy, and peace in heaven
where you live for ever and ever.

R. *Amen.*

For the solace of those present the minister may conclude these prayers with a simple blessing or with a symbolic gesture, for example, signing the forehead with the Sign of the Cross.

THE GOSPEL AND EXPLANATIONS OF THE READING

ADVENT

November 27, 2022

FIRST SUNDAY OF ADVENT

A reading from the holy Gospel according to Matthew 24:37– 44

Jesus said to his disciples:
"As it was in the days of Noah,
   so it will be at the coming of the Son of Man.
In those days before the flood,
   they were eating and drinking,
   marrying and giving in marriage,
   up to the day that Noah entered the ark.
They did not know until the flood came and carried
     them all away.
So will it be also at the coming of the Son of Man.
Two men will be out in the field;
   one will be taken, and one will be left.
Two women will be grinding at the mill;
   one will be taken, and one will be left.
Therefore, stay awake!
For you do not know on which day your Lord will come.
Be sure of this: if the master of the house
   had known the hour of night when the thief was coming,
   he would have stayed awake
   and not let his house be broken into.

So too, you also must be prepared,

for at an hour you do not expect, the Son of Man will come."

The Gospel of the Lord.

EXPLANATION OF THE READING

The Advent scriptures are filled with promise. Isaiah proclaims that the Lord will come to dwell among the chosen people. Paul tells the Roman Christians that their salvation is near at hand. Jesus tells the disciples that the coming of the Son of Man is as sure as the events in the days of their ancestors. These promises are the fulfillment of God's plan to bring salvation to all people. But the gospel text contains a warning: we must stay awake, because we do not know the time of the Lord's coming. Our vigilance is in doing the will of the Lord in the meantime.

December 4, 2022

SECOND SUNDAY OF ADVENT

A reading from the holy Gospel according to Matthew   3:1–12

John the Baptist appeared, preaching in the desert of Judea

and saying, "Repent, for the kingdom of heaven is at hand!"
It was of him that the prophet Isaiah had spoken when he said:

A voice of one crying out in the desert,
Prepare the way of the Lord,
make straight his paths.
John wore clothing made of camel's hair

and had a leather belt around his waist.
His food was locusts and wild honey.
At that time Jerusalem, all Judea,

and the whole region around the Jordan
were going out to him
and were being baptized by him in the Jordan River
as they acknowledged their sins.

When he saw many of the Pharisees and Sadducees
    coming to his baptism, he said to them, "You brood
        of vipers!
Who warned you to flee from the coming wrath?
Produce good fruit as evidence of your repentance.
And do not presume to say to yourselves,
    'We have Abraham as our father.'
For I tell you,
    God can raise up children to Abraham from these stones.
Even now the ax lies at the root of the trees.
Therefore every tree that does not bear good fruit
    will be cut down and thrown into the fire.
I am baptizing you with water, for repentance,
    but the one who is coming after me is mightier than I.
I am not worthy to carry his sandals.
He will baptize you with the Holy Spirit and fire.
His winnowing fan is in his hand.
He will clear his threshing floor
    and gather his wheat into his barn,
    but the chaff he will burn with unquenchable fire."

The Gospel of the Lord.

EXPLANATION OF THE READING

We meet John the Baptist twice during Advent. John is the great
messenger of the Messiah, the one who proclaims to a waiting world that
the promise of the ages has come to pass. In order to recognize and accept
the Messiah, John proclaims repentance. This repentance will mean
turning away from the sins of the past, their stubbornness, and infidelity
to the covenant. This call to repentance is also directed to us. We are
called to repent of whatever hinders us from receiving with our whole
being the message of the Messiah, a message of peace, mercy and justice
for all.

December 8, 2022

Solemnity of the Immaculate Conception of the Blessed Virgin Mary

A reading from the holy Gospel according to Luke   1:26–38

The angel Gabriel was sent from God
    to a town of Galilee called Nazareth,
    to a virgin betrothed to a man named Joseph,
    of the house of David,
    and the virgin's name was Mary.
And coming to her, he said,
    "Hail, full of grace! The Lord is with you."
But she was greatly troubled at what was said
    and pondered what sort of greeting this might be.
Then the angel said to her,
    "Do not be afraid, Mary,
    for you have found favor with God.
Behold, you will conceive in your womb and bear a son,
    and you shall name him Jesus.
He will be great and will be called Son of the Most High,
    and the Lord God will give him the throne of David
        his father,
    and he will rule over the house of Jacob forever,
    and of his Kingdom there will be no end."
But Mary said to the angel,
    "How can this be,
    since I have no relations with a man?"
And the angel said to her in reply,
    "The Holy Spirit will come upon you,
    and the power of the Most High will overshadow you.
Therefore the child to be born
    will be called holy, the Son of God.

And behold, Elizabeth, your relative,
   has also conceived a son in her old age,
   and this is the sixth month for her who was called barren;
   for nothing will be impossible for God."
Mary said, "Behold, I am the handmaid of the Lord.
May it be done to me according to your word."
Then the angel departed from her.

The Gospel of the Lord.

EXPLANATION OF THE READING

Luke's narrative of Gabriel's annunciation visit never fails to stir our hearts. Mary is to be the theotokos, the one who will bear the son of God to the world, fulfilling God's plan of salvation. Although we might protest that we are not as favored as Mary, we are also called to bear Christ to the world. We are to bring the light of peace and joy and hope to the world. We have been promised the gift of the Holy Spirit in our mission; a mission that God has chosen for us for "nothing will be impossible for God."

December 11, 2022

THIRD SUNDAY OF ADVENT

A reading from the holy Gospel according to Matthew   11:2–11

When John the Baptist heard in prison of the works
   of the Christ,
   he sent his disciples to Jesus with this question,
   "Are you the one who is to come,
   or should we look for another?"
Jesus said to them in reply,
   "Go and tell John what you hear and see:
   the blind regain their sight,

the lame walk,
lepers are cleansed,
the deaf hear,
the dead are raised,
and the poor have the good news proclaimed to them.
And blessed is the one who takes no offense at me."

As they were going off,
Jesus began to speak to the crowds about John,
"What did you go out to the desert to see?
A reed swayed by the wind?
Then what did you go out to see?
Someone dressed in fine clothing?
Those who wear fine clothing are in royal palaces.
Then why did you go out? To see a prophet?
Yes, I tell you, and more than a prophet.
This is the one about whom it is written:
Behold, I am sending my messenger ahead of you;
he will prepare your way before you.
Amen, I say to you,
among those born of women
there has been none greater than John the Baptist;
yet the least in the kingdom of heaven is greater than he."

The Gospel of the Lord.

EXPLANATION OF THE READING

It would be helpful to read both the Gospel and today's first reading from
Isaiah 35:1–6a. The response that Jesus gives to John's disciples echoes the
prophet's words describing the actions of the One that God will send to
save God's people. The mission of Jesus brings new life to the blind, the
lame, lepers, the deaf, the poor, and the dead. The power of God through
Jesus never fails to lift up those who are most in need of new life. We are
among those called into that new life. Whatever our situation may be,
God will not, and does not leave us without hope or redemption.

December 18, 2022

Fourth Sunday of Advent

A reading from the holy Gospel according to Matthew   1:18–24

This is how the birth of Jesus Christ came about.
When his mother Mary was betrothed to Joseph,
    but before they lived together,
    she was found with child through the Holy Spirit.
Joseph her husband, since he was a righteous man,
    yet unwilling to expose her to shame,
    decided to divorce her quietly.
Such was his intention when, behold,
    the angel of the Lord appeared to him in a dream and said,
    "Joseph, son of David,
    do not be afraid to take Mary your wife into your home.
For it is through the Holy Spirit
    that this child has been conceived in her.
She will bear a son and you are to name him Jesus,
    because he will save his people from their sins."
All this took place to fulfill what the Lord had said through
      the prophet:
    Behold, the virgin shall conceive and bear a son,
    and they shall name him Emmanuel,
    which means "God is with us."
When Joseph awoke,
    he did as the angel of the Lord had commanded him
    and took his wife into his home.

The Gospel of the Lord.

EXPLANATION OF THE READING

Throughout the Scriptures, God frequently speaks to people through the message of an angel. These messages are always life changing. The message to Joseph brings comfort, "do not be afraid." How often in our life we need to hear that message from God. Whatever the task or decision before us we want to know that we can act without fear. We may have all the facts we need, all the options available and all the support we can find, still we want the spiritual courage to move forward. It is then that we take comfort in the words of God, "do not be afraid."

CHRISTMAS TIME

December 25, 2022

SOLEMNITY OF THE NATIVITY OF THE LORD

A reading from the holy Gospel according to Luke   2:1–14

In those days a decree went out from Caesar Augustus
    that the whole world should be enrolled.
This was the first enrollment,
    when Quirinius was governor of Syria.
So all went to be enrolled, each to his own town.
And Joseph too went up from Galilee from the town
        of Nazareth
    to Judea, to the city of David that is called Bethlehem,
    because he was of the house and family of David,
    to be enrolled with Mary, his betrothed, who was with child.
While they were there,
    the time came for her to have her child,
    and she gave birth to her firstborn son.
She wrapped him in swaddling clothes and laid
        him in a manger,
    because there was no room for them in the inn.

Now there were shepherds in that region living in the fields
    and keeping the night watch over their flock.
The angel of the Lord appeared to them
    and the glory of the Lord shone around them,
    and they were struck with great fear.

The angel said to them,
  "Do not be afraid;
  for behold, I proclaim to you good news of great joy
  that will be for all the people.
For today in the city of David
  a savior has been born for you who is Christ and Lord.
And this will be a sign for you:
  you will find an infant wrapped in swaddling clothes
  and lying in a manger."
And suddenly there was a multitude of the heavenly
    host with the angel,
  praising God and saying:
    "Glory to God in the highest
        and on earth peace to those on whom his favor rests."

The Gospel of the Lord.

This reading was taken from the Mass during the Night.

EXPLANATION OF THE READING

The story of Jesus' birth never fails to engage our imagination and our emotions. Luke is a master storyteller and his details paint such a graphic picture that we imagine ourselves at the scene of Jesus' birth. We might imagine that we are friends of the family, or passers—by attracted by the commotion in a stable, or curious travelers from another place. But in the midst of our wonder we remember that this is an astonishing act of God unfolding for us. God has visited his people in the ordinariness of a birth, yet it is an extraordinary event that has changed our lives.

January 1, 2023

Solemnity of Mary, the Holy Mother of God

A reading from the holy Gospel according to Luke 2:16–21

The shepherds went in haste to Bethlehem and found Mary
        and Joseph,
    and the infant lying in the manger.
When they saw this,
    they made known the message
    that had been told them about this child.
All who heard it were amazed
    by what had been told them by the shepherds.
And Mary kept all these things,
    reflecting on them in her heart.
Then the shepherds returned,
    glorifying and praising God
    for all they had heard and seen,
    just as it had been told to them.

When eight days were completed for his circumcision,
    he was named Jesus, the name given him by the angel
    before he was conceived in the womb.

The Gospel of the Lord.

Explanation of the Reading

In the midst of Luke's narrative of the nativity of Jesus, Luke presents an image of Mary as a contemplative. Luke recounts that she "kept all these things, reflecting on them in her heart." Another translation uses the word "ponder" to describe Mary's thoughtfulness on what the birth of her child might mean. Surely every parent has such thoughts about the challenges and blessings that await their child. Mary trusts in the

Lord's favor and willingly accepts God's mission for her. She is a model for all of us, no matter what our vocation in life. May we be as trusting as she was.

January 8, 2023

Solemmity of the Epiphany of the Lord

A reading from the holy Gospel according to Matthew   2:1–12

When Jesus was born in Bethlehem of Judea,
　in the days of King Herod,
　behold, magi from the east arrived in Jerusalem, saying,
　"Where is the newborn king of the Jews?
We saw his star at its rising
　and have come to do him homage."
When King Herod heard this,
　he was greatly troubled,
　and all Jerusalem with him.
Assembling all the chief priests and the scribes of the people,
　he inquired of them where the Christ was to be born.
They said to him, "In Bethlehem of Judea,
　for thus it has been written through the prophet:
　　And you, Bethlehem, land of Judah,
　　　are by no means least among the rulers of Judah;
　　since from you shall come a ruler,
　　　who is to shepherd my people Israel."
Then Herod called the magi secretly
　and ascertained from them the time of the
　　star's appearance.
He sent them to Bethlehem and said,
　"Go and search diligently for the child.

When you have found him, bring me word,
   that I too may go and do him homage."
After their audience with the king they set out.
And behold, the star that they had seen at its rising
      preceded them,
   until it came and stopped over the place
      where the child was.
They were overjoyed at seeing the star,
   and on entering the house
   they saw the child with Mary his mother.
They prostrated themselves and did him homage.
Then they opened their treasures
   and offered him gifts of gold, frankincense, and myrrh.
And having been warned in a dream not to return to Herod,
   they departed for their country by another way.

The Gospel of the Lord.

EXPLANATION OF THE READING

Today's feast continues the celebration of the astonishing mystery of
God's manifestation to the very ends of the earth. The foreign visitors
are the messengers of this divine intervention. The attempt by Herod
to co-opt the visitors from the east into telling him the location of the
birth of Jesus does not materialize. Once again a heavenly messenger
intervenes and the Magi return home by a different route. The visitors
from the east symbolize the extent of God's salvation as it unfolds for
peoples of every land. As they offer gifts, as would be fitting a king,
they announce to the world that an astonishing event has taken place;
all peoples will know the glory of God.

Ordinary Time During Winter

January 15, 2023

Second Sunday in Ordinary Time

A reading from the holy Gospel according to John   1:29–34

John the Baptist saw Jesus coming toward him and said,
  "Behold, the Lamb of God, who takes away
    the sin of the world.
He is the one of whom I said,
  'A man is coming after me who ranks ahead of me
  because he existed before me.'
I did not know him,
  but the reason why I came baptizing with water
  was that he might be made known to Israel."
John testified further, saying,
  "I saw the Spirit come down like a dove from heaven
  and remain upon him.
I did not know him,
  but the one who sent me to baptize with water told me,
  'On whomever you see the Spirit come down and remain,
  he is the one who will baptize with the Holy Spirit.'
Now I have seen and testified that he is the Son of God."

The Gospel of the Lord.

EXPLANATION OF THE READING

John the Baptist is the herald of the One who will bring good news. John's announcement sets the stage for the ministry of Jesus as he takes up his mission of preaching forgiveness and calling his disciples to follow in his footsteps. This too is our mission: to seek the forgiveness of the Lord and to be willing to forgive with the same spirit as he did. The exclamation of John appears in our celebration of Mass as we prepare for communion: "Behold the Lamb of God, behold him who takes away the sins of the world."

January 22, 2023

THIRD SUNDAY IN ORDINARY TIME

A reading from the holy Gospel according to Matthew   4:12 – 17

When Jesus heard that John had been arrested,
　　he withdrew to Galilee.
He left Nazareth and went to live in Capernaum by the sea,
　　in the region of Zebulun and Naphtali,
　　that what had been said through Isaiah the prophet
　　might be fulfilled:
　　　Land of Zebulun and land of Naphtali,
　　　　the way to the sea, beyond the Jordan,
　　　　Galilee of the Gentiles,
　　　the people who sit in darkness have seen a great light,
　　　on those dwelling in a land overshadowed by death
　　　　light has arisen.

From that time on, Jesus began to preach and say,
  "Repent, for the kingdom of heaven is at hand."

The Gospel of the Lord.

Longer form: Matthew 4:12–23

EXPLANATION OF THE READING

Jesus' call of the first disciples marks a significant point in his mission. Matthew presents this incident as an indication that Jesus' mission will require others to help him spread the good news of the Kingdom. What is even more astounding is that these ordinary men leave their occupation and their equipment and follow Jesus. The response of Peter and the others is striking. Matthew would have us believe that Jesus' mission is so attractive that it cannot be ignored. How willing are we to do the same? What would it cost us to follow the Lord with such abandon?

January 29, 2023

FOURTH SUNDAY IN ORDINARY TIME

A reading from the holy Gospel according to Matthew   5:1–12a

When Jesus saw the crowds, he went up the mountain,
  and after he had sat down, his disciples came to him.
He began to teach them, saying:
"Blessed are the poor in spirit,
  for theirs is the kingdom of heaven.
Blessed are they who mourn,
  for they will be comforted.
Blessed are the meek,
  for they will inherit the land.
Blessed are they who hunger and thirst
    for righteousness,
  for they will be satisfied.

Blessed are the merciful,
　　for they will be shown mercy.
Blessed are the clean of heart,
　　for they will see God.
Blessed are the peacemakers,
　　for they will be called children of God.
Blessed are they who are persecuted for the sake
　　　of righteousness,
　　for theirs is the kingdom of heaven.
Blessed are you when they insult you
　　　and persecute you
　　and utter every kind of evil against you falsely because of
　　　me.
Rejoice and be glad,
　　for your reward will be great in heaven."

The Gospel of the Lord.

EXPLANATION OF THE READING

It's easy to get lost in the images of the Beatitudes and lose sight of
the challenges. Mourning is painful, but it only happens if we love.
Meekness and cleanliness of heart are not values we see on the average
television show. What models do we have to cultivate the Beatitudes?
Mercy isn't part of our world either; vengeance is much more common.
Finally, we will be persecuted. Which of the Beatitudes do you find most
challenging today?

February 5, 2023

Fifth Sunday in Ordinary Time

A reading from the holy Gospel according to Matthew   5:13–16

Jesus said to his disciples:
   "You are the salt of the earth.
But if salt loses its taste, with what can it be seasoned?
It is no longer good for anything
   but to be thrown out and trampled underfoot.
You are the light of the world.
A city set on a mountain cannot be hidden.
Nor do they light a lamp and then put it
      under a bushel basket;
   it is set on a lampstand,
   where it gives light to all in the house.
Just so, your light must shine before others,
   that they may see your good deeds
   and glorify your heavenly Father."

The Gospel of the Lord.

Explanation of the Reading

Jesus uses two domestic images, salt and light, to teach the disciples how important they are in sharing his mission. Notice that Jesus uses an emphatic phrasing: "You are . . ." Not, you can be, or you might be, or maybe you will be. No, he is very direct in naming them as salt and light, they are change agents. Just as salt adds flavor to food and light dispels the darkness, so will they transform the world by their witness and their good deeds. In accepting this identity we bring glory to God.

February 12, 2023

Sixth Sunday in Ordinary Time

**A reading from the holy Gospel
according to Matthew** 5:20–22a, 27–28, 33–34a, 37

Jesus said to his disciples:
    "I tell you, unless your righteousness surpasses
    that of the scribes and Pharisees,
    you will not enter the kingdom of heaven.

"You have heard that it was said to your ancestors,
    You shall not kill; and whoever kills will be liable
      to judgment.
But I say to you,
    whoever is angry with his brother
    will be liable to judgment.

"You have heard that it was said,
    You shall not commit adultery.
But I say to you,
    everyone who looks at a woman with lust
    has already committed adultery with her in his heart.

"Again you have heard that it was said to your ancestors,
    Do not take a false oath,
    but make good to the Lord all that you vow.
But I say to you, do not swear at all.
Let your 'Yes' mean 'Yes,' and your 'No' mean 'No.'
Anything more is from the evil one."

The Gospel of the Lord.

Longer form: Matthew 5:17–37

Explanation of the Reading

In Matthew's Gospel Jesus follows the teaching on the Beatitudes with a number of sayings that begin, "You have heard it said . . . but I say to you." In these statements Jesus teaches us that there is more to being disciples than just keeping the letter of the law. Jesus asks us to go beyond the words of the law and be attentive to any word or deed that can do harm to another. His examples are ordinary situations in life, but his teaching is rooted in kingdom thinking, not human concepts.

February 19, 2023

Seventh Sunday in Ordinary Time

A reading from the holy Gospel according to Matthew   5:38–48

Jesus said to his disciples:
   "You have heard that it was said,
   An eye for an eye and a tooth for a tooth.
But I say to you, offer no resistance to one who is evil.
When someone strikes you on your right cheek,
   turn the other one as well.
If anyone wants to go to law with you over your tunic,
   hand over your cloak as well.
Should anyone press you into service for one mile,
   go for two miles.
Give to the one who asks of you,
   and do not turn your back on one who wants to borrow.

"You have heard that it was said,
   You shall love your neighbor and hate your enemy.
But I say to you, love your enemies
   and pray for those who persecute you,
   that you may be children of your heavenly Father,

for he makes his sun rise on the bad and the good,
    and causes rain to fall on the just and the unjust.
For if you love those who love you, what recompense
      will you have?
Do not the tax collectors do the same?
And if you greet your brothers only,
    what is unusual about that?
Do not the pagans do the same?
So be perfect, just as your heavenly Father is perfect."

The Gospel of the Lord.

EXPLANATION OF THE READING

In his teaching on the Law of Moses, Jesus gives two more examples of
how disciples are to act. The issues of retribution and love of enemies are
difficult challenges for us. It is easy to desire revenge and to ignore or
even oppress those who are different from us. The Kingdom-teaching
that Jesus demands is quite different from what might be the status quo
in dealing with others. We are called to a greater law, the law of love.
We are called to attitudes and actions that see others as worthy of God's
love, and deserving of our respect and compassion.

LENT

February 26, 2023

FIRST SUNDAY OF LENT

A reading from the holy Gospel according to Matthew 4:1–11

At that time Jesus was led by the Spirit into the desert
    to be tempted by the devil.
He fasted for forty days and forty nights,
    and afterwards he was hungry.
The tempter approached and said to him,
    "If you are the Son of God,
    command that these stones become loaves of bread."
He said in reply,
    "It is written:
        One does not live on bread alone,
            but on every word that comes forth
            from the mouth of God."

Then the devil took him to the holy city,
    and made him stand on the parapet of the temple,
    and said to him, "If you are the Son of God,
        throw yourself down.
For it is written:
        He will command his angels concerning you
            and with their hands they will support you,
        lest you dash your foot against a stone."

Jesus answered him,
    "Again it is written,
    You shall not put the Lord, your God, to the test."
Then the devil took him up to a very high mountain,
    and showed him all the kingdoms of the world in
        their magnificence,
    and he said to him, "All these I shall give to you,
    if you will prostrate yourself and worship me."
At this, Jesus said to him,
    "Get away, Satan!
It is written:
    The Lord, your God, shall you worship
        and him alone shall you serve."

Then the devil left him and, behold,
    angels came and ministered to him.

The Gospel of the Lord.

EXPLANATION OF THE READING

No matter how hard we try to avoid temptations, they find their way
into our spiritual life. It seems as though they lie in wait for us, trying
to catch us when we least expect them, or when our resolve to avoid
them is weak. The story of Jesus' temptations in the desert gives us hope.
His response to the tempter came from a realization that his mission
was from God, and not from the attractions offered by the devil. In the
face of temptation, our strength comes from remembering our true self,
a son or daughter of God. Nothing is greater than that.

March 5, 2023

SECOND SUNDAY OF LENT

A reading from the holy Gospel according to Matthew 17:1–9

Jesus took Peter, James, and John his brother,
    and led them up a high mountain by themselves.
And he was transfigured before them;
    his face shone like the sun
    and his clothes became white as light.
And behold, Moses and Elijah appeared to them,
    conversing with him.
Then Peter said to Jesus in reply,
    "Lord, it is good that we are here.
If you wish, I will make three tents here,
    one for you, one for Moses, and one for Elijah."
While he was still speaking, behold,
    a bright cloud cast a shadow over them,
    then from the cloud came a voice that said,
    "This is my beloved Son, with whom I am well pleased;
    listen to him."
When the disciples heard this, they fell prostrate
    and were very much afraid.
But Jesus came and touched them, saying,
    "Rise, and do not be afraid."
And when the disciples raised their eyes,
    they saw no one else but Jesus alone.

As they were coming down from the mountain,
    Jesus charged them,
    "Do not tell the vision to anyone
    until the Son of Man has been raised from the dead."

The Gospel of the Lord.

EXPLANATION OF THE READING

Jesus' Transfiguration marks an important turning point in his mission. When he and the three disciples come down from the mountain they set their faces toward Jerusalem. There, Jesus will endure his passion and death and be raised from the dead. These events will transform the life of all those who will be his disciples. God bestowed on Jesus an identity of "my beloved." From the moment of our Baptism, we too are named the beloved of God. The voice from the cloud urges the disciples to "listen to him." When we hear and follow the word of the Lord, we live as the beloved of God.

March 12, 2023

THIRD SUNDAY OF LENT

A reading from the holy Gospel according to John   4:5–15, 19b–26, 39a, 40–42

Jesus came to a town of Samaria called Sychar,
    near the plot of land that Jacob had given to his son Joseph.
Jacob's well was there.
Jesus, tired from his journey, sat down there at the well.
It was about noon.

A woman of Samaria came to draw water.
Jesus said to her,
    "Give me a drink."
His disciples had gone into the town to buy food.

The Samaritan woman said to him,
    "How can you, a Jew, ask me, a Samaritan woman,
        for a drink?"
—For Jews use nothing in common with Samaritans.—
Jesus answered and said to her,
    "If you knew the gift of God
    and who is saying to you, 'Give me a drink,'
    you would have asked him
    and he would have given you living water."
The woman said to him,
    "Sir, you do not even have a bucket and the cistern is deep;
    where then can you get this living water?
Are you greater than our father Jacob,
    who gave us this cistern and drank from it himself
    with his children and his flocks?"
Jesus answered and said to her,
    "Everyone who drinks this water will be thirsty again;
    but whoever drinks the water I shall give will never thirst;
    the water I shall give will become in him
    a spring of water welling up to eternal life."
The woman said to him,
    "Sir, give me this water, so that I may not be thirsty
    or have to keep coming here to draw water.

"I can see that you are a prophet.
Our ancestors worshiped on this mountain;
    but you people say that the place to worship is in Jerusalem."
Jesus said to her,
    "Believe me, woman, the hour is coming
    when you will worship the Father
    neither on this mountain nor in Jerusalem.

You people worship what you do not understand;
  we worship what we understand,
  because salvation is from the Jews.
But the hour is coming, and is now here,
  when true worshipers will worship the Father
    in Spirit and truth;
  and indeed the Father seeks such people to worship him.
God is Spirit, and those who worship him
  must worship in Spirit and truth."
The woman said to him,
  "I know that the Messiah is coming, the one called the Christ;
  when he comes, he will tell us everything."
Jesus said to her,
  "I am he, the one who is speaking with you."

Many of the Samaritans of that town began to believe in him.
When the Samaritans came to him,
  they invited him to stay with them;
  and he stayed there two days.
Many more began to believe in him because of his word,
  and they said to the woman,
  "We no longer believe because of your word;
  for we have heard for ourselves,
  and we know that this is truly the savior of the world."

The Gospel of the Lord.

Longer form: John 4:5–42

EXPLANATION OF THE READING

The encounter between Jesus and the Samaritan woman at the well is
rich in imagery and meaning. In their conversation Jesus uncovers the
spiritual thirst of the woman for "living water." In our Lenten journey,
we seek the living water of Jesus present in the proclaimed word,

in order to be refreshed over and over again in our hearts and our soul. God is imaged as a great cistern, "the cistern is deep" the woman points out. The measure of life offered by God in Jesus is beyond our imaging but not beyond our reach. This is a story of hope, of healing, and of joy. It prefigures all that Easter celebrates.

March 19, 2023

FOURTH SUNDAY OF LENT

**A reading from the holy Gospel
according to John**   9:1, 6–9, 13–17, 34–38

As Jesus passed by he saw a man blind from birth.
He spat on the ground and made clay with the saliva,
   and smeared the clay on his eyes, and said to him,
   "Go wash in the Pool of Siloam"—which means Sent—.
So he went and washed, and came back able to see.

His neighbors and those who had seen him earlier
    as a beggar said,
   "Isn't this the one who used to sit and beg?"
Some said, "It is,"
   but others said, "No, he just looks like him."
He said, "I am."

They brought the one who was once blind to the Pharisees.
Now Jesus had made clay and opened his eyes on a sabbath.
So then the Pharisees also asked him how he was able to see.
He said to them,
   "He put clay on my eyes, and I washed, and now I can see."

So some of the Pharisees said,
    "This man is not from God,
    because he does not keep the sabbath."
But others said,
    "How can a sinful man do such signs?"
And there was a division among them.
So they said to the blind man again,
    "What do you have to say about him,
    since he opened your eyes?"
He said, "He is a prophet."

They answered and said to him,
    "You were born totally in sin,
    and are you trying to teach us?"
Then they threw him out.

When Jesus heard that they had thrown him out,
    he found him and said, "Do you believe in the Son of Man?"
He answered and said,
    "Who is he, sir, that I may believe in him?"
Jesus said to him,
    "You have seen him,
    and the one speaking with you is he."
He said,
    "I do believe, Lord," and he worshiped him.

The Gospel of the Lord.

Longer form: John 9:1–41

EXPLANATION OF THE READING

The healing of the man born blind is the second of the great stories from John's account of the Gospel for our Lenten reflection. The intervention of Jesus in a human disability is another indication of the power of God that works through Jesus and brings healing to the man born blind and skepticism among the crowd of onlookers. Jesus turns their religious belief upside down. In stating that neither the man nor his parents have sinned, Jesus reveals that the mercy of God comes to those who believe that Jesus is Lord.

March 26, 2023

Fifth Sunday of Lent

A reading from the holy Gospel according to John   11:3–7, 17, 20–27, 33b–45

The sisters of Lazarus sent word to Jesus, saying,
   "Master, the one you love is ill."
When Jesus heard this he said,
   "This illness is not to end in death,
   but is for the glory of God,
   that the Son of God may be glorified through it."
Now Jesus loved Martha and her sister and Lazarus.
So when he heard that he was ill,
   he remained for two days in the place where he was.
Then after this he said to his disciples,
   "Let us go back to Judea."

When Jesus arrived, he found that Lazarus
   had already been in the tomb for four days.
When Martha heard that Jesus was coming,
   she went to meet him;
   but Mary sat at home.
Martha said to Jesus,
   "Lord, if you had been here,
   my brother would not have died.

But even now I know that whatever you ask of God,
    God will give you."
Jesus said to her,
    "Your brother will rise."
Martha said,
    "I know he will rise,
    in the resurrection on the last day."
Jesus told her,
    "I am the resurrection and the life;
    whoever believes in me, even if he dies, will live,
    and everyone who lives and believes in me will never die.
Do you believe this?"
She said to him, "Yes, Lord.
I have come to believe that you are the Christ,
    the Son of God,
    the one who is coming into the world."

He became perturbed and deeply troubled, and said,
    "Where have you laid him?"
They said to him, "Sir, come and see."
And Jesus wept.
So the Jews said, "See how he loved him."
But some of them said,
    "Could not the one who opened the eyes of the blind man
    have done something so that this man would not have died?"

So Jesus, perturbed again, came to the tomb.
It was a cave, and a stone lay across it.
Jesus said, "Take away the stone."
Martha, the dead man's sister, said to him,
    "Lord, by now there will be a stench;
    he has been dead for four days."

Jesus said to her,
   "Did I not tell you that if you believe
   you will see the glory of God?"
So they took away the stone.
And Jesus raised his eyes and said,
   "Father, I thank you for hearing me.
I know that you always hear me;
   but because of the crowd here I have said this,
   that they may believe that you sent me."
And when he had said this,
   He cried out in a loud voice,
   "Lazarus, come out!"
The dead man came out,
   tied hand and foot with burial bands,
   and his face was wrapped in a cloth.
So Jesus said to them,
   "Untie him and let him go."

Now many of the Jews who had come to Mary
   and seen what he had done began to believe in him.

The Gospel of the Lord.

Longer form: John 11:1–45

EXPLANATION OF THE READING

The raising of Lazarus from the dead prefigures Jesus' own Resurrection. This third in the collection of John's stories in which Jesus reveals his divine identity also sets the stage for his own death. Although many come to believe in him, the religious leaders regard his actions as blasphemous. The intimacy of the relationship that Jesus has with Mary, Martha, and their brother Lazarus can overshadow the astonishing action of Jesus. He reveals himself as the "the resurrection and the life." This is our hope, this is our faith. We too will be raised from the dead.

April 2, 2023

Palm Sunday of the Passion of the Lord

A reading from the holy Gospel according to Matthew   21:1–11

When Jesus and the disciples drew near Jerusalem
    and came to Bethphage on the Mount of Olives,
    Jesus sent two disciples, saying to them,
    "Go into the village opposite you,
    and immediately you will find an ass tethered,
    and a colt with her.
Untie them and bring them here to me.
And if anyone should say anything to you, reply,
    'The master has need of them.'
Then he will send them at once."
This happened so that what had been spoken through
     the prophet
   might be fulfilled:
     Say to daughter Zion,
     "Behold, your king comes to you,
      meek and riding on an ass,
      and on a colt, the foal of a beast of burden."
The disciples went and did as Jesus had ordered them.
They brought the ass and the colt and laid their cloaks
     over them,
   and he sat upon them.
The very large crowd spread their cloaks on the road,
    while others cut branches from the trees
    and strewed them on the road.

The crowds preceding him and those following
    kept crying out and saying:
        "Hosanna to the Son of David;
            blessed is he who comes in the name of the Lord;
        hosanna in the highest."
And when he entered Jerusalem
    the whole city was shaken and asked, "Who is this?"
And the crowds replied,
    "This is Jesus the prophet, from Nazareth in Galilee."

The Gospel of the Lord.

EXPLANATION OF THE READING

As Jesus enters the city of Jerusalem we want to be there with the crowds,
shouting our acclamations and sharing in his glory. Matthew's description
of this amazing event makes it clear that Jesus is in charge. He sends his
disciples to make arrangements for the procession into the city; the crowds
respond with cries of adoration. Even as this joyous event draws us into
its unfolding, we know that Jesus' passion and death will soon follow.
But for today, we want to acclaim Jesus as our Lord and share in the glory
of this prophet from Nazareth.

This Gospel reading was taken from the blessing of the palms.

EASTER TIME

April 9, 2023

EASTER SUNDAY OF THE RESURRECTION OF THE LORD

A reading from the holy Gospel according to John   20:1–9

On the first day of the week,
  Mary of Magdala came to the tomb early in the morning,
  while it was still dark,
  and saw the stone removed from the tomb.
So she ran and went to Simon Peter
  and to the other disciple whom Jesus loved, and told them,
  "They have taken the Lord from the tomb,
  and we don't know where they put him."
So Peter and the other disciple went out and came
    to the tomb.
They both ran, but the other disciple ran faster than Peter
  and arrived at the tomb first;
  he bent down and saw the burial cloths there,
    but did not go in.
When Simon Peter arrived after him,
  he went into the tomb and saw the burial cloths there,
  and the cloth that had covered his head,
  not with the burial cloths but rolled up in a separate place.
Then the other disciple also went in,
  the one who had arrived at the tomb first,
  and he saw and believed.

For they did not yet understand the Scripture
   that he had to rise from the dead.

The Gospel of the Lord.

Explanation of the Reading

On this Easter day we accompany Mary of Magdala to the tomb. What are
we looking for this day? An Easter party with great singing and flowers
and Easter bonnets? Surely we can ask more of ourselves. I think we want
more and we desire to embrace more than the surface, the obvious, and
the easy. The message of the resurrection is the gift of freedom; freedom
from a death that would mark the end; freedom from the bonds of
remorse, of cynicism, of despair. Resurrection is also the gift of being
free to make choices we've never made before: to pray, to love, to forgive,
to hope, to enjoy.

April 16, 2023

Second Sunday of Easter
(or Sunday of Divine Mercy)

A reading from the holy Gospel according to John   20:19 – 31

On the evening of that first day of the week,
   when the doors were locked, where the disciples were,
   for fear of the Jews,
   Jesus came and stood in their midst
   and said to them, "Peace be with you."
When he had said this, he showed them his hands and his side.
The disciples rejoiced when they saw the Lord.
Jesus said to them again, "Peace be with you.
As the Father has sent me, so I send you."
And when he had said this, he breathed on them
      and said to them,
   "Receive the Holy Spirit.

Whose sins you forgive are forgiven them,
and whose sins you retain are retained."

Thomas, called Didymus, one of the Twelve,
was not with them when Jesus came.
So the other disciples said to him, "We have seen the Lord."
But he said to them,
"Unless I see the mark of the nails in his hands
and put my finger into the nailmarks
and put my hand into his side, I will not believe."

Now a week later his disciples were again inside
and Thomas was with them.
Jesus came, although the doors were locked,
and stood in their midst and said, "Peace be with you."
Then he said to Thomas, "Put your finger here
and see my hands,
and bring your hand and put it into my side,
and do not be unbelieving, but believe."
Thomas answered and said to him, "My Lord
and my God!"
Jesus said to him, "Have you come to believe because you
have seen me?
Blessed are those who have not seen and have believed."

Now, Jesus did many other signs in the presence
of his disciples
that are not written in this book.
But these are written that you may come to believe
that Jesus is the Christ, the Son of God,
and that through this belief you may have life in his name.

The Gospel of the Lord.

EXPLANATION OF THE READING

The account of Thomas' doubt overshadows the other experience in today's reading, namely the gathering of the disciples "on the first day of the week." This is an image of our gathering within our own parish communities. Like the first disciples, we need each other to believe and to celebrate that belief. We are truly the signs and wonders of Christ the risen Lord in the world. Our catechumens came to faith because of others who were witnesses of the Lord. Even when we doubt, the witness of others strengthens our hope and renews the peace Christ promised.

April 23, 2023

THIRD SUNDAY OF EASTER

A reading from the holy Gospel according to Luke   24:13–35

That very day, the first day of the week,
  two of Jesus' disciples were going
  to a village seven miles from Jerusalem called Emmaus,
  and they were conversing about all the things
    that had occurred.
And it happened that while they were conversing
    and debating,
  Jesus himself drew near and walked with them,
  but their eyes were prevented from recognizing him.
He asked them,
  "What are you discussing as you walk along?"
They stopped, looking downcast.
One of them, named Cleopas, said to him in reply,
  "Are you the only visitor to Jerusalem
  who does not know of the things
  that have taken place there in these days?"
And he replied to them, "What sort of things?"

They said to him,
    "The things that happened to Jesus the Nazarene,
    who was a prophet mighty in deed and word
    before God and all the people,
    how our chief priests and rulers both handed him over
    to a sentence of death and crucified him.
But we were hoping that he would be the one to redeem Israel;
    and besides all this,
    it is now the third day since this took place.
Some women from our group, however, have astounded us:
    they were at the tomb early in the morning
    and did not find his body;
    they came back and reported
    that they had indeed seen a vision of angels
    who announced that he was alive.
Then some of those with us went to the tomb
    and found things just as the women had described,
    but him they did not see."
And he said to them, "Oh, how foolish you are!
How slow of heart to believe all that the prophets spoke!
Was it not necessary that the Christ should suffer these things
    and enter into his glory?"
Then beginning with Moses and all the prophets,
    he interpreted to them what referred to him
    in all the Scriptures.
As they approached the village to which they were going,
    he gave the impression that he was going on farther.
But they urged him, "Stay with us,
    for it is nearly evening and the day is almost over."
So he went in to stay with them.

And it happened that, while he was with them at table,
  he took bread, said the blessing,
  broke it, and gave it to them.
With that their eyes were opened and they recognized him,
  but he vanished from their sight.
Then they said to each other,
  "Were not our hearts burning within us
  while he spoke to us on the way and opened the
    Scriptures to us?"
So they set out at once and returned to Jerusalem
  where they found gathered together
  the eleven and those with them who were saying,
  "The Lord has truly been raised and has appeared to Simon!"
Then the two recounted
  what had taken place on the way
  and how he was made known to them
    in the breaking of bread.

The Gospel of the Lord.

EXPLANATION OF THE READING

The story of Emmaus begins and ends with a journey, as does our Sunday experience. Walking with family and friends, neighbors and other parishioners, we are always accompanied by another presence, the risen Lord. To sense that presence, to be conscious of the Lord himself walking with us, is the beginning of a Eucharistic experience. When the word of God is proclaimed, we are invited to see our life in a new light. When we come to the table of the Lord for the breaking of the bread we are made ready to continue the journey with hearts filled with the fire of his love.

April 30, 2023

Fourth Sunday of Easter

A reading from the holy Gospel according to John 10:1–10

Jesus said:
    "Amen, amen, I say to you,
      whoever does not enter a sheepfold through the gate
      but climbs over elsewhere is a thief and a robber.
But whoever enters through the gate is the shepherd
      of the sheep.
The gatekeeper opens it for him, and the sheep hear his voice,
      as the shepherd calls his own sheep by name
      and leads them out.
When he has driven out all his own,
      he walks ahead of them, and the sheep follow him,
      because they recognize his voice.
But they will not follow a stranger;
      they will run away from him,
      because they do not recognize the voice of strangers."
Although Jesus used this figure of speech,
      the Pharisees did not realize what he was trying to tell them.

So Jesus said again, "Amen, amen, I say to you,
      I am the gate for the sheep.
All who came before me are thieves and robbers,
      but the sheep did not listen to them.
I am the gate.
Whoever enters through me will be saved,
      and will come in and go out and find pasture.

A thief comes only to steal and slaughter and destroy;
   I came so that they might have life and have it
      more abundantly."

The Gospel of the Lord.

Explanation of the Reading

There are several aspects associated with the image of Jesus as the Good Shepherd. In today's reading, Jesus portrays himself not as the shepherd but as the gate, the door to the sheep fold, the place where the sheep are housed and protected. It was customary for the shepherd to sleep in the entrance of the sheepfold to provide security for the sheep against predators or thieves. Jesus' self-portrait assures us of his unconditional love for us. What better comfort could we have than his promise that he has come among us so that we "might have life and have it more abundantly" (John 10:10)?

May 7, 2023

Fifth Sunday of Easter

A reading from the holy Gospel according to John   14:1–12

Jesus said to his disciples:
   "Do not let your hearts be troubled.
You have faith in God; have faith also in me.
In my Father's house there are many dwelling places.
If there were not,
   would I have told you that I am going to prepare
      a place for you?
And if I go and prepare a place for you,
   I will come back again and take you to myself,
   so that where I am you also may be.
Where I am going you know the way."

Thomas said to him,
  "Master, we do not know where you are going;
  how can we know the way?"
Jesus said to him, "I am the way and the truth and the life.
No one comes to the Father except through me.
If you know me, then you will also know my Father.
From now on you do know him and have seen him."
Philip said to him,
  "Master, show us the Father, and that will
    be enough for us."
Jesus said to him, "Have I been with you for so long a time
  and you still do not know me, Philip?
Whoever has seen me has seen the Father.
How can you say, 'Show us the Father'?
Do you not believe that I am in the Father and
    the Father is in me?
The words that I speak to you I do not speak on my own.
The Father who dwells in me is doing his works.
Believe me that I am in the Father and the Father is in me,
  or else, believe because of the works themselves.
Amen, amen, I say to you,
  whoever believes in me will do the works that I do,
  and will do greater ones than these,
  because I am going to the Father."

The Gospel of the Lord.

EXPLANATION OF THE READING

When we were young, we asked our parents or our teachers, "Where is God?" This is the question from Thomas in today's Gospel. As adult believers, we have come to understand that the "where-ness" of God is not so much God's private address but an "awareness" of God that is about presence. The message of Jesus to the disciples is that God dwells within the household of believers just as Jesus is in their midst.

Divine presence is a household of many dwelling places, many rooms. In other words, God is big enough to live in the whole community of believers, wherever they are.

May 14, 2023

SIXTH SUNDAY OF EASTER

A reading from the holy Gospel according to John   14:15–21

Jesus said to his disciples:
  "If you love me, you will keep my commandments.
And I will ask the Father,
  and he will give you another Advocate
    to be with you always,
  the Spirit of truth, whom the world cannot accept,
  because it neither sees nor knows him.
But you know him, because he remains with you,
  and will be in you.
I will not leave you orphans; I will come to you.
In a little while the world will no longer see me,
  but you will see me, because I live and you will live.
On that day you will realize that I am in my Father
  and you are in me and I in you.
Whoever has my commandments and observes them
  is the one who loves me.
And whoever loves me will be loved by my Father,
  and I will love him and reveal myself to him."

The Gospel of the Lord.

EXPLANATION OF THE READING

Some of the most heart-wrenching images that appear after natural disasters or in the midst of war are those of children. They are victims of natural disasters, armed aggression, famine, and human neglect; they are orphans. When Jesus uses this image in the Gospel, it tells us that he understands the anxiety of the human family. Like a solicitous parent, he consoles his disciples, assuring them that he will not abandon them in their fear and anxiety. He promises them, and us, that he will remain among us in a new way. Together we continue to shape his mission by our lives.

May 18 or May 21, 2023

SOLEMNITY OF THE ASCENSION OF THE LORD

A reading from the holy Gospel according to Matthew   28:16–20

The eleven disciples went to Galilee,
   to the mountain to which Jesus had ordered them.
When they saw him, they worshiped, but they doubted.
Then Jesus approached and said to them,
   "All power in heaven and on earth has been given to me.
Go, therefore, and make disciples of all nations,
   baptizing them in the name of the Father,
   and of the Son, and of the Holy Spirit,
   teaching them to observe all that I have commanded you.
And behold, I am with you always, until the end of the age."

The Gospel of the Lord.

EXPLANATION OF THE READING

It is easy to get stuck in the literalism of the Ascension—Jesus "lifting off" from earth like a rocket! Today's solemnity purposely takes us away from the literal. We celebrate Jesus being glorified and going to the right hand of the Father. He commissions us and then bodily departs, so that, "Christ has no body but yours, no hands, no feet on earth but yours. . . . Yours are the hands, yours are the feet, yours are the eyes, you are his body. Christ has no body now but yours" (St. Teresa of Avila). "Go, therefore, and make disciples of all nations."

May 21, 2023

Seventh Sunday of Easter

A reading from the holy Gospel according to John   17:1–11a

Jesus raised his eyes to heaven and said,
   "Father, the hour has come.
Give glory to your son, so that your son may glorify you,
   just as you gave him authority over all people,
   so that your son may give eternal life to all you gave him.
Now this is eternal life,
   that they should know you, the only true God,
   and the one whom you sent, Jesus Christ.
I glorified you on earth
   by accomplishing the work that you gave me to do.
Now glorify me, Father, with you,
   with the glory that I had with you before the world began.

"I revealed your name to those whom you gave me
      out of the world.
They belonged to you, and you gave them to me,
   and they have kept your word.
Now they know that everything you gave me is from you,
   because the words you gave to me I have given to them,
   and they accepted them and truly understood
      that I came from you,
   and they have believed that you sent me.
I pray for them.
I do not pray for the world but for the ones you have given me,
   because they are yours, and everything of mine is yours
   and everything of yours is mine,
   and I have been glorified in them.

And now I will no longer be in the world,
but they are in the world, while I am coming to you."

The Gospel of the Lord.

EXPLANATION OF THE READING

Chapter 17 of John's account of the Gospel is often referred to as the priestly prayer of Jesus. His words are addressed to the Father; he prays for his disciples, the ones the Father gave him. It is one of the most beautiful passages in John's Gospel, portraying the tender and personal feelings of Jesus for his followers. We could adopt Jesus' thoughts for ourselves, seeing ourselves as those that the Father has placed in the company of his Son, chosen to be his followers, his friends. When Jesus says, "I pray for them," we can imagine that he prays also for us. What a wonderful blessing.

May 28, 2023

SOLEMNITY OF PENTECOST

A reading from the holy Gospel according to John   20:19 – 23

On the evening of that first day of the week,
when the doors were locked, where the disciples were,
for fear of the Jews,
Jesus came and stood in their midst
and said to them, "Peace be with you."
When he had said this, he showed them his hands
and his side.
The disciples rejoiced when they saw the Lord.
Jesus said to them again, "Peace be with you.
As the Father has sent me, so I send you."

And when he had said this, he breathed on them
    and said to them,
  "Receive the Holy Spirit.
Whose sins you forgive are forgiven them,
    and whose sins you retain are retained."

The Gospel of the Lord.

EXPLANATION OF THE READING

We could say that the Resurrection is about us looking at the work of
God. Pentecost is God looking at us through the gift of the Spirit.
Pentecost means that we cannot stand looking up to the heavens, like
the disciples at the Ascension. Pentecost means that it is time to engage
life and to shape the Kingdom of God; to put flesh and bones, hands and
feet on the teachings of Christ. Pentecost means that each of us
possesses gifts that come from the Spirit and together those gifts enrich
and build up the Body of Christ in the world.

Ordinary Time during the Summer and Fall

June 4, 2023

Solemnity of the Most Holy Trinity

A reading from the holy Gospel according to John 3:16–18

God so loved the world that he gave his only Son,
   so that everyone who believes in him might not perish
   but might have eternal life.
For God did not send his Son into the world
    to condemn the world,
   but that the world might be saved through him.
Whoever believes in him will not be condemned,
   but whoever does not believe has already been condemned,
   because he has not believed in the name
    of the only Son of God.

The Gospel of the Lord.

Explanation of the Reading

The Scriptures reveal that the Father, Son, and Holy Spirit cannot be understood apart from their unity. To be in a relationship with God is to enter a relationship with all that God is and all that God does. Our union with God is a union of concern for all God has created. We are initiated into that union at Baptism, and at that moment we no longer exist in isolation but are joined with the communion of saints; we become members of a body that we dare to name the Body of Christ. Every time we invoke the Trinitarian God we affirm this truth.

June 11, 2023

Solemnity of the Most Holy Body and Blood of Christ (Corpus Christi)

A reading from the holy Gospel according to John   6:51–58

Jesus said to the Jewish crowds:
    "I am the living bread that came down from heaven;
    whoever eats this bread will live forever;
    and the bread that I will give
    is my flesh for the life of the world."

The Jews quarreled among themselves, saying,
    "How can this man give us his flesh to eat?"
Jesus said to them,
    "Amen, amen, I say to you,
    unless you eat the flesh of the Son of Man
        and drink his blood,
    you do not have life within you.
Whoever eats my flesh and drinks my blood
    has eternal life,
    and I will raise him on the last day.
For my flesh is true food,
    and my blood is true drink.
Whoever eats my flesh and drinks my blood
    remains in me and I in him.
Just as the living Father sent me
    and I have life because of the Father,
    so also the one who feeds on me
    will have life because of me.
This is the bread that came down from heaven.
Unlike your ancestors who ate and still died,
    whoever eats this bread will live forever."

The Gospel of the Lord.

Explanation of the Reading

At every Eucharist we accept and commit to a Christ like relationship with all those who join us at the altar, and with all those we encounter in life. Our concern is different than the crowds who ask: "How can this man give us his flesh to eat?" Our concern is how to give what we have and who we are to those who hunger and thirst for God. Our faith assures us that Jesus is the living bread for us; it is that same faith that sends us from Eucharist to be living loaves of love, bearers of justice and signs of compassion.

June 18, 2023

Eleventh Sunday in Ordinary Time

A reading from the holy Gospel according to Matthew   9:36—10:8

At the sight of the crowds, Jesus' heart was moved with pity
    for them
  because they were troubled and abandoned,
  like sheep without a shepherd.
Then he said to his disciples,
    "The harvest is abundant but the laborers are few;
    so ask the master of the harvest
    to send out laborers for his harvest."

Then he summoned his twelve disciples
and gave them authority over unclean spirits
to drive them out and to cure every disease and every illness.
The names of the twelve apostles are these:
    first, Simon called Peter, and his brother Andrew;
    James, the son of Zebedee, and his brother John;
    Philip and Bartholomew, Thomas and Matthew the
        tax collector;

James, the son of Alphaeus, and Thaddeus;
Simon from Cana, and Judas Iscariot who betrayed him.
Jesus sent out these twelve after instructing them thus,
"Do not go into pagan territory or enter a Samaritan town.
Go rather to the lost sheep of the house of Israel.
As you go, make this proclamation: 'The kingdom of heaven
    is at hand.'
Cure the sick, raise the dead, cleanse lepers, drive
    out demons.
Without cost you have received; without cost you are to give."

The Gospel of the Lord.

EXPLANATION OF THE READING

Throughout Jesus' public ministry, his acts of healing draw mixed reactions from those around him. Often the religious authorities consider his actions as blasphemy, while the crowds are amazed and come to believe in him. Today's incident is an example of both. But Jesus is undeterred. Matthew tells us "his heart was moved with pity for them because they were troubled and abandoned, like sheep without a shepherd." When we come before the Lord with our many needs in life we can be assured that the Lord looks kindly on us as well. He is our good shepherd.

June 25, 2023

TWELFTH SUNDAY IN ORDINARY TIME

A reading from the holy Gospel according to Matthew   10:26–33

Jesus said to the Twelve:
"Fear no one.
Nothing is concealed that will not be revealed,
    nor secret that will not be known.

What I say to you in the darkness, speak in the light;
   what you hear whispered, proclaim on the housetops.
And do not be afraid of those who kill the body
      but cannot kill the soul;
   rather, be afraid of the one who can destroy
   both soul and body in Gehenna.
Are not two sparrows sold for a small coin?
Yet not one of them falls to the ground
      without your Father's knowledge.
Even all the hairs of your head are counted.
So do not be afraid; you are worth more than many sparrows.
Everyone who acknowledges me before others
   I will acknowledge before my heavenly Father.
But whoever denies me before others,
   I will deny before my heavenly Father."

The Gospel of the Lord.

EXPLANATION OF THE READING

It seems to be part of human nature to fear the unknown. As a child, it might have been the darkness; as an adult it may be any unfamiliar event or task that is in our future. Jesus addresses the Twelve as a parent might console a child. He encourages his followers to put their trust in his word and in his friendship for them. He assures them that the Father's love is as tender as that for a sparrow, and as deliberate as knowing the number of hairs on their head. Strange comparisons, but we are that precious in the sight of God.

July 2, 2023

THIRTEENTH SUNDAY IN ORDINARY TIME

A reading from the holy Gospel according to Matthew 10:37–42

Jesus said to his apostles:
    "Whoever loves father or mother more than me is
        not worthy of me,
    and whoever loves son or daughter more than me is
        not worthy of me;
    and whoever does not take up his cross
    and follow after me is not worthy of me.
Whoever finds his life will lose it,
    and whoever loses his life for my sake will find it.

"Whoever receives you receives me,
    and whoever receives me receives the one who sent me.
Whoever receives a prophet because he is a prophet
    will receive a prophet's reward,
    and whoever receives a righteous man
    because he is a righteous man
    will receive a righteous man's reward.
And whoever gives only a cup of cold water
    to one of these little ones to drink
    because the little one is a disciple—
    amen, I say to you, he will surely not lose his reward."

The Gospel of the Lord.

EXPLANATION OF THE READING

At first glance, today's reading seems a little harsh. Jesus seems to be saying that we should set aside love of parents and siblings or else we are not worthy of his love for us. The key word is more. Jesus exhorts us to place our love for him above all others, but not instead of others. In fact, when we read the Gospel carefully we discover that we come to love the Lord through others, and we love others because of the Lord. It is an integrated love affair that we have with the Lord; it is a wonderful grace that we cannot live without!

July 9, 2023

Fourteenth Sunday in Ordinary Time

A reading from the holy Gospel according to Matthew   11:25–30

At that time Jesus exclaimed:
"I give praise to you, Father, Lord of heaven and earth,
　　for although you have hidden these things
　　from the wise and the learned
　　you have revealed them to little ones.
Yes, Father, such has been your gracious will.
All things have been handed over to me by my Father.
No one knows the Son except the Father,
　　and no one knows the Father except the Son
　　and anyone to whom the Son wishes to reveal him.

"Come to me, all you who labor and are burdened,
　　and I will give you rest.
Take my yoke upon you and learn from me,
　　for I am meek and humble of heart;
　　and you will find rest for yourselves.
For my yoke is easy, and my burden light."

The Gospel of the Lord.

Explanation of the Reading

For Jesus "the little ones" are those who are not so full of their own wisdom that they are oblivious to the revelations of God. Like children, they are always open to learning and are amazed at what can help them to grow in understanding the world around them. These are the people that Jesus invites to hear his word and to come to know the Father. Even when they might find that difficult, he assures them, and us, that his "burden is light." In other words, he is always there to help us, to walk with us, and to share our journey.

July 16, 2023

FIFTEENTH SUNDAY IN ORDINARY TIME

A reading from the holy Gospel according to Matthew 13:1–9

On that day, Jesus went out of the house
    and sat down by the sea.
Such large crowds gathered around him
    that he got into a boat and sat down,
    and the whole crowd stood along the shore.
And he spoke to them at length in parables, saying:
    "A sower went out to sow.
And as he sowed, some seed fell on the path,
    and birds came and ate it up.
Some fell on rocky ground, where it had little soil.
It sprang up at once because the soil was not deep,
    and when the sun rose it was scorched,
    and it withered for lack of roots.
Some seed fell among thorns, and the thorns grew up
        and choked it.
But some seed fell on rich soil and produced fruit,
    a hundred or sixty or thirtyfold.
Whoever has ears ought to hear."

The Gospel of the Lord.

Longer form: Matthew 13:1–23

Explanation of the Reading

Jesus was fond of using parables with agricultural imagery. The sowing of seed on various types of land is one of his favorites. It is the only one that he actually explains. The seed is the "word of the kingdom" and the soil is likened to those who hear the word. Sometimes the word takes root in our lives and sometimes it doesn't. Sometimes it lasts for only a short while and sometimes it flourishes and produces a harvest of good works. The latter reality is always our task; the word of God shapes our discipleship and brings life to the world.

July 23, 2023

Sixteenth Sunday in Ordinary Time

A reading from the holy Gospel according to Matthew 13:24–30

Jesus proposed another parable to the crowds, saying:
"The kingdom of heaven may be likened to a man
    who sowed good seed in his field.
While everyone was asleep his enemy came
    and sowed weeds all through the wheat, and then went off.
When the crop grew and bore fruit, the weeds
        appeared as well.
The slaves of the householder came to him and said,
    'Master, did you not sow good seed in your field?
Where have the weeds come from?'
He answered, 'An enemy has done this.'
His slaves said to him, 'Do you want us to go
        and pull them up?'
He replied, 'No, if you pull up the weeds
    you might uproot the wheat along with them.
Let them grow together until harvest;
    then at harvest time I will say to the harvesters,

"First collect the weeds and tie them in bundles for burning; but gather the wheat into my barn."""

The Gospel of the Lord.

Longer form: Matthew 13:24–43

EXPLANATION OF THE READING

This passage shows how gently Jesus deals with his people. The wheat and the weeds are growing together, and Jesus does not want to uproot one from the other. Sometimes we are eager to judge what is good and what is bad; however, those are not always so identifiable. Perhaps we need to allow ourselves to be tender with all and let the good come to fruition. Openness to mercy while an individual matures can encourage virtue to flourish.

July 30, 2023

SEVENTEENTH SUNDAY IN ORDINARY TIME

A reading from the holy Gospel according to Matthew 13:44–46

Jesus said to his disciples:
"The kingdom of heaven is like a treasure buried in a field,
which a person finds and hides again,
and out of joy goes and sells all that he has
and buys that field.
Again, the kingdom of heaven is like a merchant
searching for fine pearls.
When he finds a pearl of great price,
he goes and sells all that he has and buys it."

The Gospel of the Lord.

Longer form: Matthew 13:44–52

EXPLANATION OF THE READING

Jesus continues to teach his disciples, and us, about the Kingdom of God by using parables and images that we easily understand. Who among us would not want to find a great treasure? Maybe we are thinking of winning the lottery! Or, what would it be like to find a rare pearl? In both cases, we would be excited and surely want to share our good fortune with others. The kingdom of heaven is the treasure, the pearl. It is given to us by God, no digging, no ticket required. It is pure gift. And it is meant to be shared with great joy.

August 6, 2023

FEAST OF THE TRANSIFGURATION OF THE LORD

A reading from the holy Gospel according to Matthew   17:1–9

Jesus took Peter, James, and John his brother,
   and led them up a high mountain by themselves.
And he was transfigured before them;
   his face shone like the sun
   and his clothes became white as light.
And behold, Moses and Elijah appeared to them,
   conversing with him.
Then Peter said to Jesus in reply,
   "Lord, it is good that we are here.
If you wish, I will make three tents here,
   one for you, one for Moses, and one for Elijah."
While he was still speaking, behold,
   a bright cloud cast a shadow over them,
   then from the cloud came a voice that said,
   "This is my beloved Son, with whom I am well pleased;
   listen to him."
When the disciples heard this, they fell prostrate
   and were very much afraid.

But Jesus came and touched them, saying,
  "Rise, and do not be afraid."
And when the disciples raised their eyes,
  they saw no one else but Jesus alone.

As they were coming down from the mountain,
  Jesus charged them,
  "Do not tell the vision to anyone
  until the Son of Man has been raised from the dead."

The Gospel of the Lord.

EXPLANATION OF THE READING

The Transfiguration of Jesus marks a turning point in his public ministry. The presence of Moses and Elijah indicates that Jesus stands in the great tradition of the law and the prophets, the two principal vehicles of God's plan of salvation. But Jesus must embrace his part in that plan and move toward Jerusalem where he will suffer, die and rise from the dead. His disciples will walk with him on that journey. We are called to accompany Jesus; only then will we be transformed and share in his glory.

August 13, 2023

NINETEENTH SUNDAY IN ORDINARY TIME

A reading from the holy Gospel according to Matthew 14:22 – 33

After he had fed the people, Jesus made the disciples
    get into a boat
  and precede him to the other side,
  while he dismissed the crowds.
After doing so, he went up on the mountain by himself to pray.
When it was evening he was there alone.

Meanwhile the boat, already a few miles offshore,
    was being tossed about by the waves, for the wind
        was against it.
During the fourth watch of the night,
    he came toward them walking on the sea.
When the disciples saw him walking on the sea they
        were terrified.
"It is a ghost," they said, and they cried out in fear.
At once Jesus spoke to them, "Take courage, it is I;
        do not be afraid."
Peter said to him in reply,
    "Lord, if it is you, command me to come to you
        on the water."
He said, "Come."
Peter got out of the boat and began to walk
        on the water toward Jesus.
But when he saw how strong the wind was he
        became frightened;
    and, beginning to sink, he cried out, "Lord, save me!"
Immediately Jesus stretched out his hand and caught Peter,
    and said to him, "O you of little faith, why did you doubt?"
After they got into the boat, the wind died down.
Those who were in the boat did him homage, saying,
    "Truly, you are the Son of God."

The Gospel of the Lord.

EXPLANATION OF THE READING

The encounters between Jesus and Peter are always intriguing. Peter's
humanness appeals to us. In today's story, he wants to walk on the water
like Jesus, but he loses his nerve and begins to sink. There may be
something of Peter in each of us. Deep in our heart we want to follow
the Lord, yet there are moments when we vacillate and wonder if we can
believe everything the Lord teaches and everything he asks of us.

In those moments we can lose our nerve, or renew our faith and cry out, "Lord, save me." And he always does.

August 15, 2023

Solemnity of the Assumption of the Blessed Virgin Mary

A reading from the holy Gospel according to Luke   1:39–56

Mary set out
and traveled to the hill country in haste
to a town of Judah,
where she entered the house of Zechariah
and greeted Elizabeth.
When Elizabeth heard Mary's greeting,
the infant leaped in her womb,
and Elizabeth, filled with the Holy Spirit,
cried out in a loud voice and said,
"Blessed are you among women,
and blessed is the fruit of your womb.
And how does this happen to me,
that the mother of my Lord should come to me?
For at the moment the sound of your greeting reached my ears,
the infant in my womb leaped for joy.
Blessed are you who believed
that what was spoken to you by the Lord
would be fulfilled."

And Mary said:

"My soul proclaims the greatness of the Lord;
    my spirit rejoices in God my Savior
    for he has with favor on his lowly servant.
From this day all generations will call me blessed:
    the Almighty has done great things for me
    and holy is his Name.
    He has mercy on those who fear him
    in every generation.
He has shown the strength of his arm,
    and has scattered the proud in their conceit.
He has cast down the mighty from their thrones,
    and has lifted up the lowly.
He has filled the hungry with good things,
    and the rich he has sent away empty.
He has come to the help of his servant Israel
    for he has remembered his promise of mercy,
    the promise he made to our fathers,
    to Abraham and his children forever."

Mary remained with her about three months
    and then returned to her home.

The Gospel of the Lord.

EXPLANATION OF THE READING

There are only a few accounts of Mary found in the Gospel. On a couple of occasions Jesus refers to his family, and today's reading is one of those. A woman gives praise for the mother of Jesus who gave him life. This is a worthy compliment, and Jesus accepts the comment as an opportunity to extend his notion of family to all those who hear the Word of God. His mission is not confined to his immediate family; he has a greater household to establish, one that is united by the power and grace of the Word of God.

August 20, 2023

Twentieth Sunday in Ordinary Time

A reading from the holy Gospel according to Matthew 15:21–28

At that time, Jesus withdrew to the region of Tyre and Sidon.
And behold, a Canaanite woman of that district came
    and called out,
  "Have pity on me, Lord, Son of David!
My daughter is tormented by a demon."
But Jesus did not say a word in answer to her.
Jesus' disciples came and asked him,
  "Send her away, for she keeps calling out after us."
He said in reply,
"I was sent only to the lost sheep of the house of Israel."
But the woman came and did Jesus homage, saying,
    "Lord, help me."
He said in reply,
  "It is not right to take the food of the children
  and throw it to the dogs."
She said, "Please, Lord, for even the dogs eat the scraps
  that fall from the table of their masters."
Then Jesus said to her in reply,
  "O woman, great is your faith!
Let it be done for you as you wish."
And the woman's daughter was healed from that hour.

The Gospel of the Lord.

Explanation of the Reading

The Canaanite woman represents those who were considered to be both socially and religiously outsiders. Her persistence annoyed the disciples who wanted to send her away. But her persistence gets Jesus' attention.

She humbly acknowledges that she doesn't deserve the same kindness that others receive, but still she begs for a few scraps of love, a simple healing for her daughter. Jesus is moved by her great faith and grants her request. We are never outside the reach of Jesus' compassion. When we come with humility and faith he will not turn us away.

August 27, 2023

Twenty-First Sunday in Ordinary Time

A reading from the holy Gospel according to Matthew   16:13–20

Jesus went into the region of Caesarea Philippi and
   he asked his disciples,
   "Who do people say that the Son of Man is?"
They replied, "Some say John the Baptist, others Elijah,
   still others Jeremiah or one of the prophets."
He said to them, "But who do you say that I am?"
Simon Peter said in reply,
   "You are the Christ, the Son of the living God."
Jesus said to him in reply,
   "Blessed are you, Simon son of Jonah.
For flesh and blood has not revealed this to you,
   but my heavenly Father.
And so I say to you, you are Peter,
   and upon this rock I will build my church,
   and the gates of the netherworld shall not prevail against it.
I will give you the keys to the kingdom of heaven.
Whatever you bind on earth shall be bound in heaven;
   and whatever you loose on earth shall be loosed in heaven."
Then he strictly ordered his disciples
   to tell no one that he was the Christ.

The Gospel of the Lord.

Explanation of the Reading

The Church has long regarded this passage as the foundational moment for the establishment of the ministry of the pope as head of the Church. The symbol of keys appears in the papal crest, the sign both of governance and of leadership that is rooted in the person of Jesus Christ. Peter, the rock, symbolizes that the human community that is the Church, rests on the permanence of its divine foundation. Although Jesus commissions Peter to a ministry of reconciliation, that same mandate is given to all his disciples. The strength of the Church depends on a communion of love, justice, and mercy.

September 3, 2023

Twenty-Second Sunday in Ordinary Time

A reading from the holy Gospel according to Matthew 16:21–27

Jesus began to show his disciples
   that he must go to Jerusalem and suffer greatly
   from the elders, the chief priests, and the scribes,
   and be killed and on the third day be raised.
Then Peter took Jesus aside and began to rebuke him,
   "God forbid, Lord! No such thing shall ever happen to you."
He turned and said to Peter,
   "Get behind me, Satan! You are an obstacle to me.
You are thinking not as God does, but as human beings do."

Then Jesus said to his disciples,
   "Whoever wishes to come after me must deny himself,
   take up his cross, and follow me.
For whoever wishes to save his life will lose it,
   but whoever loses his life for my sake will find it.

What profit would there be for one to gain the whole world
  and forfeit his life?
Or what can one give in exchange for his life?
For the Son of Man will come with his angels
    in his Father's glory,
  and then he will repay all according to his conduct."

The Gospel of the Lord.

EXPLANATION OF THE READING

Today's reading presents another interesting conversation between Jesus and Peter. Not only is Peter unwilling to go to Jerusalem where suffering awaits, he doesn't want Jesus to go either. Jesus has already said that he will endure suffering and death, and now he is prepared to undergo this fate. This encounter with Peter allows him to teach us what it takes to follow him and what it means for our salvation. Taking up our cross may not lead to the kind of death and suffering that Jesus endured, but it does mean that whatever our cross might be, it will be the way to gain eternal life with Jesus.

September 10, 2023

TWENTY-THIRD SUNDAY IN ORDINARY TIME

A reading from the holy Gospel according to Matthew   18:15–20

Jesus said to his disciples:
  "If your brother sins against you,
  go and tell him his fault between you and him alone.
If he listens to you, you have won over your brother.

If he does not listen,
    take one or two others along with you,
    so that 'every fact may be established
    on the testimony of two or three witnesses.'
If he refuses to listen to them, tell the church.
If he refuses to listen even to the church,
    then treat him as you would a Gentile or a tax collector.
Amen, I say to you,
    whatever you bind on earth shall be bound in heaven,
    and whatever you loose on earth shall be loosed in heaven.
Again, amen, I say to you,
    if two of you agree on earth
    about anything for which they are to pray,
    it shall be granted to them by my heavenly Father.
For where two or three are gathered together in my name,
    there am I in the midst of them."

The Gospel of the Lord.

EXPLANATION OF THE READING

The exercise of forgiveness can often be difficult. Whether we seek forgiveness in the Sacrament of Penance or attempt to be reconciled with someone whom we have hurt, it can be an emotional struggle. Jesus' exhortation in today's reading describes reconciliation as both an individual act and a communal practice. When someone sins against us, we are called upon to meet that person face to face. If that does not lead to reconciliation, we should involve others who can help to restore a bond of communion. However, the first step is a desire in our heart to be reconciled, to restore peace and to live in freedom from our sin.

September 17, 2023

TWENTY-FOURTH SUNDAY IN ORDINARY TIME

A reading from the holy Gospel according to Matthew   18:21–35

Peter approached Jesus and asked him,
  "Lord, if my brother sins against me,
   how often must I forgive?
As many as seven times?"
Jesus answered, "I say to you, not seven times
      but seventy-seven times.
That is why the kingdom of heaven may be likened to a king
   who decided to settle accounts with his servants.
When he began the accounting,
   a debtor was brought before him who owed him
      a huge amount.
Since he had no way of paying it back,
   his master ordered him to be sold,
   along with his wife, his children, and all his property,
   in payment of the debt.
At that, the servant fell down, did him homage, and said,
   'Be patient with me, and I will pay you back in full.'
Moved with compassion the master of that servant
   let him go and forgave him the loan.
When that servant had left, he found one of his fellow servants
   who owed him a much smaller amount.
He seized him and started to choke him, demanding,
   'Pay back what you owe.'
Falling to his knees, his fellow servant begged him,
   'Be patient with me, and I will pay you back.'
But he refused.

Instead, he had the fellow servant put in prison
    until he paid back the debt.
Now when his fellow servants saw what had happened,
    they were deeply disturbed, and went to their master
    and reported the whole affair.
His master summoned him and said to him,
        'You wicked servant!
I forgave you your entire debt because you begged me to.
Should you not have had pity on your fellow servant,
    as I had pity on you?'
Then in anger his master handed him over to the torturers
    until he should pay back the whole debt.
So will my heavenly Father do to you,
    unless each of you forgives your brother from your heart."

The Gospel of the Lord.

Explanation of the Reading

The question that Peter asks Jesus about the number of times one must forgive another may well be our question! After all, just how often should I be expected to forgive someone who keeps sinning against me? The Law of Moses had stipulated that three times was enough, and Peter appears to be generous in asking if seven times is sufficient. Jesus' response must have shocked him. Jesus is not giving him a lesson in math but in mercy. The unconditional and forgiving love of the Father is the example for the disciples of Jesus. This teaching is at the heart of the parable of the unforgiving servant that follows this reading (see Matthew 18:21–35).

September 24, 2023

TWENTY-FIFTH SUNDAY IN ORDINARY TIME

A reading from the holy Gospel according to Matthew   20:1–16a

Jesus told his disciples this parable:
  "The kingdom of heaven is like a landowner
  who went out at dawn to hire laborers for his vineyard.
After agreeing with them for the usual daily wage,
  he sent them into his vineyard.
Going out about nine o'clock,
  the landowner saw others standing idle in the marketplace,
  and he said to them, 'You too go into my vineyard,
  and I will give you what is just.'
So they went off.
And he went out again around noon,
  and around three o'clock, and did likewise.
Going out about five o'clock,
  the landowner found others standing around,
    and said to them,
  'Why do you stand here idle all day?'
They answered, 'Because no one has hired us.'
He said to them, 'You too go into my vineyard.'
When it was evening the owner of the vineyard said
    to his foreman,
  'Summon the laborers and give them their pay,
  beginning with the last and ending with the first.'
When those who had started about five o'clock came,
  each received the usual daily wage.

So when the first came, they thought that they would
    receive more,
  but each of them also got the usual wage.
And on receiving it they grumbled against the
    landowner, saying,
  'These last ones worked only one hour,
  and you have made them equal to us,
  who bore the day's burden and the heat.'
He said to one of them in reply,
  'My friend, I am not cheating you.
Did you not agree with me for the usual daily wage?
Take what is yours and go.
What if I wish to give this last one the same as you?
Or am I not free to do as I wish with my own money?
Are you envious because I am generous?'
Thus, the last will be first, and the first will be last."

The Gospel of the Lord.

EXPLANATION OF THE READING

Today's reading is one of several in Matthew's account of the Gospel known as the Kingdom parables. The full parable includes the master's choice to pay all the workers the same wage. The first part of the parable tells us that the Lord invites whomever he chooses to work in his vineyard. The labor of all who are invited is needed, just as the gifts of all are needed, for the work of the Kingdom. The choice is the Lord's, not ours. So too, the reward of discipleship is not governed by our sense of fairness but by the generosity of the Lord. We are grateful to be invited.

October 1, 2023

Twenty-Sixth Sunday in Ordinary Time

A reading from the holy Gospel according to Matthew   21:28–32

Jesus said to the chief priests and elders of the people:
  "What is your opinion?
A man had two sons.
He came to the first and said,
  'Son, go out and work in the vineyard today.'
He said in reply, 'I will not,'
  but afterwards changed his mind and went.
The man came to the other son and gave the same order.
He said in reply, 'Yes, sir,' but did not go.
Which of the two did his father's will?"
They answered, "The first."
Jesus said to them, "Amen, I say to you,
  tax collectors and prostitutes
  are entering the kingdom of God before you.
When John came to you in the way of righteousness,
  you did not believe him;
  but tax collectors and prostitutes did.
Yet even when you saw that,
  you did not later change your minds and believe him."

The Gospel of the Lord.

Explanation of the Reading

We change our minds all the time! Jesus uses this common human trait to condemn the chief priests and elders for their failure to accept the Kingdom of God. He compares them to the son who agreed to do the father's will but then did not. The other son is compared to the tax collectors and prostitutes who repented of their ways and came to believe in God. It is a harsh judgement; but it underlines both the arrogance of the religious leaders and the availability of God's mercy. God gives us every opportunity to accept the invitation to be his servants.

October 8, 2023

TWENTY-SEVENTH SUNDAY IN ORDINARY TIME

A reading from the holy Gospel according to Matthew 21:33–43

Jesus said to the chief priests and the elders of the people:
  "Hear another parable.
There was a landowner who planted a vineyard,
  put a hedge around it, dug a wine press in it,
    and built a tower.
Then he leased it to tenants and went on a journey.
When vintage time drew near,
  he sent his servants to the tenants to obtain his produce.
But the tenants seized the servants and one they beat,
  another they killed, and a third they stoned.
Again he sent other servants, more numerous
    than the first ones,
  but they treated them in the same way.
Finally, he sent his son to them, thinking,
  'They will respect my son.'
But when the tenants saw the son, they said to one another,
  'This is the heir.
Come, let us kill him and acquire his inheritance.'
They seized him, threw him out of the vineyard,
    and killed him.
What will the owner of the vineyard do to those tenants when
    he comes?"

They answered him,

"He will put those wretched men to a wretched death
and lease his vineyard to other tenants
who will give him the produce at the proper times."
Jesus said to them, "Did you never read in the Scriptures:

The stone that the builders rejected
    has become the cornerstone;
by the Lord has this been done,
    and it is wonderful in our eyes?
Therefore, I say to you,
the kingdom of God will be taken away from you
and given to a people that will produce its fruit."

The Gospel of the Lord.

Explanation of the Reading

Some of Jesus' parables are a little dense when it comes to understanding the message hidden within them. But today's parable is very clearly a judgement against the people of Israel and their religious leaders for not recognizing that Jesus comes from God. Sometimes our own agendas can blind us from recognizing the word and work of the Lord right in our midst. We set our hearts on a personal goal or way of doing things. Jesus reminds us that we always need to leave room for the ways of God.

October 15, 2023

Twenty-Eighth Sunday in Ordinary Time

A reading from the holy Gospel according to Matthew   22:1–10

Jesus again in reply spoke to the chief priests
    and elders of the people
    in parables, saying,

"The kingdom of heaven may be likened to a king
who gave a wedding feast for his son.
He dispatched his servants
to summon the invited guests to the feast,
but they refused to come.
A second time he sent other servants, saying,
'Tell those invited: "Behold, I have prepared my banquet,
my calves and fattened cattle are killed,
and everything is ready; come to the feast."'
Some ignored the invitation and went away,
one to his farm, another to his business.
The rest laid hold of his servants,
mistreated them, and killed them.
The king was enraged and sent his troops,
destroyed those murderers, and burned their city.
Then he said to his servants, 'The feast is ready,
but those who were invited were not worthy to come.
Go out, therefore, into the main roads
and invite to the feast whomever you find.'
The servants went out into the streets
and gathered all they found, bad and good alike,
and the hall was filled with guests."

The Gospel of the Lord.

Longer form: Matthew 22:1–14

EXPLANATION OF THE READING

It is considered an honor to be invited to a wedding feast. We are being
asked to participate in an important event in another person's life, and to
share their joy and their blessings. Presumably, they have a high regard for
our friendship and our presence. To refuse, much less ignore, such an
invitation is simply not very good manners. When the friendship that is
being celebrated is between us and God, then the obligation to respond

is considerably more serious. The parable invites the question: What is more important than participating in the love and life of Jesus Christ?

October 22, 2023

Twenty-Ninth Sunday in Ordinary Time

A reading from the holy Gospel according to Matthew   22:15–21

The Pharisees went off
   and plotted how they might entrap Jesus in speech.
They sent their disciples to him, with the Herodians, saying,
   "Teacher, we know that you are a truthful man
   and that you teach the way of God in accordance
     with the truth.
And you are not concerned with anyone's opinion,
   for you do not regard a person's status.
Tell us, then, what is your opinion:
   Is it lawful to pay the census tax to Caesar or not?"
Knowing their malice, Jesus said,
   "Why are you testing me, you hypocrites?
Show me the coin that pays the census tax."
Then they handed him the Roman coin.
He said to them, "Whose image is this
    and whose inscription?"
They replied, "Caesar's."
At that he said to them,
   "Then repay to Caesar what belongs to Caesar
   and to God what belongs to God."

The Gospel of the Lord.

EXPLANATION OF THE READING

The Pharisees attempted to trap Jesus with their questions on several occasions. And each time they lost. Or rather, Jesus turned the tables on them, and they ended up bringing judgement on themselves. Paying taxes to Caesar was a sore point for the Jewish people who were under the rule of the Romans. But it was a law of the time and people were subject to the law. But they were also subjects of God, and Jesus indicates that they could be faithful to God and still be good citizens. Placing God first was just as important for them, as it is for us, in all things.

October 29, 2023

THIRTIETH SUNDAY IN ORDINARY TIME

A reading from the holy Gospel according to Matthew 22:34 – 40

When the Pharisees heard that Jesus had silenced
    the Sadducees,
  they gathered together, and one of them,
  a scholar of the law, tested him by asking,
  "Teacher, which commandment in the law is the greatest?"
He said to him,
"You shall love the Lord, your God,
  with all your heart,
  with all your soul,
  and with all your mind.
This is the greatest and the first commandment.
The second is like it:
  You shall love your neighbor as yourself.
The whole law and the prophets depend on these
    two commandments."

The Gospel of the Lord.

Explanation of the Reading

Once again, the Pharisees try to entrap Jesus with a question about the Law of Moses. Given the many laws in the Torah, over six hundred, it would seem logical to ask which one is the greatest. Jesus' response is much more than a law; it is the basis for keeping every law. If love of God and love of neighbor is at the heart of every act and every word that shape a person's behavior, then they are truly faithful to the law of God. To love God and to love neighbor is one and the same; therein lies the way of faith and salvation.

November 1, 2023

Solemnity of All Saints

A reading from the holy Gospel according to Matthew 5:1–12a

When Jesus saw the crowds, he went up the mountain,
  and after he had sat down, his disciples came to him.
He began to teach them, saying:

> "Blessed are the poor in spirit,
>   for theirs is the Kingdom of heaven.
> Blessed are they who mourn,
>   for they will be comforted.
> Blessed are the meek,
>   for they will inherit the land.
> Blessed are they who hunger and thirst for righteousness,
>   for they will be satisfied.
> Blessed are the merciful,
>   for they will be shown mercy.
> Blessed are the clean of heart,
>   for they will see God.

Blessed are the peacemakers,
> for they will be called children of God.

Blessed are they who are persecuted for the sake
> of righteousness,
> for theirs is the Kingdom of heaven.

Blessed are you when they insult you and persecute you
> and utter every kind of evil against you falsely
> > because of me.

Rejoice and be glad,
> for your reward will be great in heaven."

The Gospel of the Lord.

EXPLANATION OF THE READING

The Beatitudes comprise one of the most familiar and most beloved texts of the Gospel. For Matthew, they act as the foundation of Jesus' mission. For Jesus, they offer a twofold message. First, they announce a present blessing. The poor in spirit—those who mourn, those who are merciful, etc.—are already blessed. God has indeed favored them. Second, the Beatitudes place a future challenge before the followers of Jesus; they are called on to recognize the blessings of God and to strive to live in such a way as to receive the same blessings.

November 5, 2023

THIRTY-FIRST SUNDAY IN ORDINARY TIME

A reading from the holy Gospel according to Matthew   23:1–12

Jesus spoke to the crowds and to his disciples, saying,
> "The scribes and the Pharisees
> have taken their seat on the chair of Moses.

Therefore, do and observe all things whatsoever they tell you,
> but do not follow their example.

For they preach but they do not practice.
They tie up heavy burdens hard to carry
    and lay them on people's shoulders,
    but they will not lift a finger to move them.
All their works are performed to be seen.
They widen their phylacteries and lengthen their tassels.
They love places of honor at banquets,
        seats of honor in synagogues,
    greetings in marketplaces, and the salutation 'Rabbi.'
As for you, do not be called 'Rabbi.'
You have but one teacher, and you are all brothers.
Call no one on earth your father;
    you have but one Father in heaven.
Do not be called 'Master';
    you have but one master, the Christ.
The greatest among you must be your servant.
Whoever exalts himself will be humbled;
    but whoever humbles himself will be exalted.'"

The Gospel of the Lord.

EXPLANATION OF THE READING

Listening to Jesus rail against the Pharisees can lead us into
self-righteousness. After all, it is easy to use the failings of others as an
excuse to ignore or reject what they represent, especially if that teaching
is a challenge to us. The Pharisees were holy men. They erred by
considering faith a body of prohibitions, warnings, and threats. Pope
Francis has reminded us that we must show that the Good News really
is cause for joy.

November 12, 2023

Thirty-Second Sunday in Ordinary Time

A reading from the holy Gospel according to Matthew   25:1–13

Jesus told his disciples this parable:
   "The kingdom of heaven will be like ten virgins
    who took their lamps and went out to meet
     the bridegroom.
Five of them were foolish and five were wise.
The foolish ones, when taking their lamps,
    brought no oil with them,
    but the wise brought flasks of oil with their lamps.
Since the bridegroom was long delayed,
    they all became drowsy and fell asleep.
At midnight, there was a cry,
    'Behold, the bridegroom! Come out to meet him!'
Then all those virgins got up and trimmed their lamps.
The foolish ones said to the wise,
    'Give us some of your oil,
    for our lamps are going out.'
But the wise ones replied,
    'No, for there may not be enough for us and you.
Go instead to the merchants and buy some for yourselves.'
While they went off to buy it,
    the bridegroom came
    and those who were ready went into the wedding feast
     with him.
Then the door was locked.
Afterwards the other virgins came and said,
    'Lord, Lord, open the door for us!'

But he said in reply,
    'Amen, I say to you, I do not know you.'
Therefore, stay awake,
    for you know neither the day nor the hour."

The Gospel of the Lord.

EXPLANATION OF THE READING

Although the season of Advent is three weeks away, the Scripture readings at this time of the year begin to give hints of the themes that Advent will proclaim. One of those is preparedness. The parable of the ten bridesmaids is an example of being prepared for the coming of the Son of God. We could read this parable about being ready for our death, but it is also a reminder to us that the Lord moves in our life at all times. We always need to be attentive to his grace that nourishes our daily life.

November 19, 2023

THIRTY-THIRD SUNDAY IN ORDINARY TIME

A reading from the holy Gospel according to Matthew   25:14–15, 19–21

Jesus told his disciples this parable:
"A man going on a journey
    called in his servants and entrusted his possessions to them.
To one he gave five talents; to another, two; to a third, one—
    to each according to his ability.
Then he went away.

"After a long time
  the master of those servants came back
  and settled accounts with them.
The one who had received five talents came forward
  bringing the additional five.
He said, 'Master, you gave me five talents.
See, I have made five more.'
His master said to him, 'Well done, my good
    and faithful servant.
Since you were faithful in small matters,
  I will give you great responsibilities.
Come, share your master's joy.'"

The Gospel of the Lord.

Longer form: Matthew 25:14–30

EXPLANATION OF THE READING

Like most parables, this one has more than one interpretation. The talents
could be considered the gifts that God gives us to use fruitfully in life.
Or the talents might be a symbol of our astuteness and stewardship of
the resources we have managed to accumulate in life. Yet another
interpretation is seeing the trust that God places in us in the first place.
After all, it is God's Kingdom with which we have been entrusted. God
"goes on a journey," leaving us to do God's work. What a privilege! And we
take care of God's gifts, not because we have to, but because we want to.

November 26, 2023

Solemnity of Our Lord Jesus Christ, King of the Universe

A reading from the holy Gospel according to Matthew 25:31–46

Jesus said to his disciples:
  "When the Son of Man comes in his glory,
  and all the angels with him,
  he will sit upon his glorious throne,
  and all the nations will be assembled before him.
And he will separate them one from another,
  as a shepherd separates the sheep from the goats.
He will place the sheep on his right and the goats on his left.
Then the king will say to those on his right,
  'Come, you who are blessed by my Father.
Inherit the kingdom prepared for you
    from the foundation of the world.
For I was hungry and you gave me food,
  I was thirsty and you gave me drink,
  a stranger and you welcomed me,
  naked and you clothed me,
  ill and you cared for me,
  in prison and you visited me.'
Then the righteous will answer him and say,
  'Lord, when did we see you hungry and feed you,
  or thirsty and give you drink?
When did we see you a stranger and welcome you,
  or naked and clothe you?
When did we see you ill or in prison, and visit you?'

And the king will say to them in reply,
  'Amen, I say to you, whatever you did
  for one of the least brothers of mine, you did for me.'
Then he will say to those on his left,
  'Depart from me, you accursed,
  into the eternal fire prepared for the devil and his angels.
For I was hungry and you gave me no food,
  I was thirsty and you gave me no drink,
  a stranger and you gave me no welcome,
  naked and you gave me no clothing,
  ill and in prison, and you did not care for me.'
Then they will answer and say,
  'Lord, when did we see you hungry or thirsty
  or a stranger or naked or ill or in prison,
  and not minister to your needs?'
He will answer them, 'Amen, I say to you,
  what you did not do for one of these least ones,
  you did not do for me.'
And these will go off to eternal punishment,
  but the righteous to eternal life."

The Gospel of the Lord.

EXPLANATION OF THE READING

Matthew's account of the Last Judgement never fails to cause us to
seriously examine our behavior as disciples of Jesus. The words of
Jesus—as often as you did this, or did not do this, to one of the least
ones, you did it to me—cut through all our excuses and any spiritual
smugness we might have. The needs of our brothers and sisters are as
prevalent today as in the time of Jesus. Each of us can recall examples
of when we responded, and when we did not reach out. This reading
could well be our daily examination of conscience.

Patron Saints

The saints and blesseds are our companions in prayer on our journey with Christ. Here we provide you with a list of health concerns and the saints chosen to intercede on a sick person's behalf before God the Father.

ILLNESS	SAINT(S)
A abdominal pains	Agapitus; Charles Borromeo; Emerentiana; Erasmus; Liborius
abortion, protection against	Catherine of Sweden
abuse victims	Adelaide; Agostina Pietrantoni; Fabiola; John Baptist de la Salle; Germaine Cousin; Godelieve; Jeanne de Lestonnac; Jeanne Marie de Maille; Joaquina Vedruna de Mas; Laura Vicuna; Maria Bagnesi; Monica; Rita of Cascia
AIDS patients	Aloysius Gonzaga; Thérèse of Lisieux; Peregrine Lazios
alcoholism	John of God; Martin of Tours; Matthias the Apostle; Monica; Urban of Langres
angina sufferers	Swithbert
appendicitis	Erasmus (Elmo)
apoplexy, apoplexies, stroke, stroke victims	Andrew Avellino; Wolfgang
arm pain; pain in the arms	Amalburga
B babies	The Holy Innocents; Maximus; Nicholas of Tolentino; Philip of Zell
bacterial disease and infection	Agrippina
barren women	Anthony of Padua; Felicity
barrenness, against	Agatha; Anne; Anthony of Padua; Casilda of Toledo; Felicity; Fiacre; Francis of Paola; Giles; Henry II; Margaret of Antioch; Philomena; Rita of Cascia; Theobald Roggeri

birth complications, against	Ulric	
birth pains	Erasmus	
blind people, blindness	Catald; Cosmas and Damian; Dunstan; Lawrence the Illuminator; Leodegarius; Lucy; Lutgardis; Odila; Parasceva; Raphael the Archangel; Thomas the Apostle	
blood donors	Our Lady of the Thorns	
bodily ills, illness, sickness	Alphais; Alphonsa of India; Angela Merici; Angela Truszkowska; Arthelais; Bathild; Bernadette of Lourdes; Camillus of Lellis; Catherine del Ricci; Catherine of Siena; Drogo; Edel Quinn; Elizabeth of the Trinity; Germaine Cousin; Hugh of Lincoln; Isabella of France; Jacinta Marto; John of God; Julia Billiart; Julia Falconieri; Juliana of Nicomedia; Louis IX; Louise de Marillac; Lydwina of Schiedam; Maria Bagnesi; Maria Gabriella; Maria Mazzarello; Marie Rose Durocher; Mary Ann de Paredes; Mary Magdalen of Pazzi; Michael the Archangel; Our Lady of Lourdes; Paula Frassinetti; Peregrine Laziosi; Philomena; Rafka Al-Rayes; Raphael; Teresa of Avila; Teresa Valse Pantellini; Terese of the Andes; Thérèse of Lisieux	
breast cancer	Agatha; Aldegundis; Giles; Peregrine	
breast disease, against	Agatha	
breastfeeding women	Giles	
broken bones	Drogo; Stanislaus Kostka	
C cancer patients; against cancer	Aldegundis; Giles; James Salomone; Peregrine Laziosi	
child abuse victims	Alodia; Germaine Cousin; Lufthild; Nunilo	
childbirth	Erasmus; Gerard Majella; Leonard of Noblac; Lutgardis; Margaret (or Marina) of Antioch; Raymond Nonnatus	

childhood diseases	Aldegundis; Pharaildis
childhood intestinal diseases	Erasmus
children, convulsive	Guy of Anderlecht; John the Baptist; Scholastica
children, death of	Alphonsa Hawthorne; Angela of Foligno; Clotilde; Conception Cabrera de Annida; Cyriacus of Iconium; Elizabeth of Hungary; Elizabeth Ann Seton; Felicity; Frances of Rome; Hedwig; Isidore the Farmer; Joaquina Vedruna de Mas; Leopold the Good; Louis IX; Margaret of Scotland; Marguerite d'Youville; Matilda; Melania the Younger; Michelina; Nonna; Perpetua; Stephen of Hungary
children, sick	Beuno; Clement I; Hugh of Lincoln; Ubaldus Baldassini
children, stammering	Notkar Balbulus
colic	Agapitus; Charles Borromeo; Emerentiana; Erasmus; Liborius
contagious diseases	Robert Bellarmine; Sebastian
consumption	Pantaleon; Thérèse of Lisieux
convulsions	John the Baptist; Willibrord
coughs, against	Blase; Quentin; Walburga
cramps, against	Cadoc of Llancarvan; Maurice; Pancras
cures from pain	Madron
D deaf people, deafness	Cadoc of Llancarvan; Drogo; Francis de Sales; Meriadoc; Ouen
death	Michael the Archangel; Margaret (or Marina) of Antioch
death, happy	Joseph; Ulric
death, against sudden	Aldegundis; Andrew Avellino; Barbara; Christopher
disabled, handicapped	Alphais; Angela Merici; Gerald of Aurillac; Germaine Cousin; Giles;

		Henry II; Lutgardis; Margaret of Castello; Seraphina; Servatus; Servulus
	drug abuse	Maximillian Kolbe
	dying people, invoked by	Abel; Barbara; Benedict; Catherine of Alexandria; James the Lesser, Apostle; John of God; Joseph; Margaret (or Marina) of Antioch; Michael the Archangel; Nicholas of Tolentino; Sebastian
	dysentary	Lucy of Syracuse; Polycarp
E	earache, against	Cornelius; Polycarp of Smyrna
	epidemics	Godeberta; Lucy of Syracuse; Our Lady of Zapopan; Roch (Rocco)
	epilepsy, epileptics	Alban of Mainz; Anthony the Abbot; Balthasar; Bibiana; Catald; Christopher; Cornelius; Dymphna; Genesius; Gerard of Lunel; Giles; Guy of Anderlecht; John Chrysostom; John the Baptist; Valentine; Vitus; Willibrord
	ergotism, aginst	Anthony the Abbot
	erysipelas	Anthony the Abbot; Benedict; Ida of Nivelles
	expectant mothers	Gerard Majella; Raymond Nonnatus
	eyes, eye diseases, eye problems, sore eyes	Aloysius Gonzaga; Augustine of Hippo; Clare of Assisi; Cyriacus of Iconium; Erhard of Regensburg; Herve; Leodegarius; Lucy of Syracuse; Raphael the Archangel; Symphorian of Autun
F	fainting, faintness	Urban of Langres; Ursus of Ravenna; Valentine
	fever, against	Abraham; Adalard; Amalberga; Andrew Abellon; Antoninus of Florence; Benedict; Castorus; Claudius; Cornelius; Dominic of Sora; Domitian of Huy; Genevieve; Gerebernus; Gertrude of Nivelles; Hugh of Cluny; Liborius; Mary of Oignies; Peter the Apostle; Petronilla; Raymond Nonnatus; Severus of Avranches;

		Sigismund; Theobald Roggeri; Ulric; Winnoc
	fistula	Fiacre
	frenzy, against	Denis; Peter the Apostle; Ulric
	foot problems; feet problems	Peter the Apostle; Servatus
G	gall stones	Benedict; Drogo; Florentius of Strasburg; Liborius
	goiter	Blase
	gout, against; gout sufferers	Andrew the Apostle; Coloman; Gregory the Great; Killian; Maurice
H	hangovers	Bibiana
	head injuries	John Licci
	headaches	Anastasius the Persian; Bibiana; Denis; Dionysius the Aeropagite; Gerard of Lunel; Gereon; Pancras; Stephen the Martyr; Teresa of Avila
	health	Infant Jesus of Prague
	healthy throats	Andrew the Apostle; Blase; Etheldreda; Godelieve; Ignatius of Antioch; Lucy of Syracuse; Swithbert
	heart patients	John of God
	hemorrhage	Lucy
	hemorrhoid, piles	Fiacre
	hernia	Alban of Mainz; Condrad Piacenzai; Cosmas and Damian; Drogo; Gummarus
	herpes	George
	hoarseness, against	Bernadine of Sienna; Maurus
	hydrophobia (rabies)	Dominic de Silos; Guy of Anderlecht; Hubert of Liege; Otto of Bamberg; Sithney; Walburga
I	infectious diseases	Edmund; Rocco
	infertility, against	Agatha; Anne; Anthony of Padua; Casilda of Toledo; Felicity; Fiacre; Francis of

		Paola; Giles; Henry II; Margaret of Antioch; Philomena; Rita of Cascia
	inflammatory disease	Benedict
	intestinal diseases, against	Brice; Charles Borromeo; Emerentiana; Erasmus; Timothy; Wolfgang
	invalids, homebound	Roch (Rocco)
J	jaundice	Odilo
K	kidney disease, against	Benedict; Drogo; Margaret (or Marina) of Antioch; Ursus of Ravenna
	kidney stones; gravel	Alban of Mainz
	knee diseases or trouble	Roch (Rocco)
L	lame, the	Giles
	leg diseases, leg trouble	Servatus
	lepers, leprosy	George; Giles; Lazarus; Vincent de Paul
	long life	Peter the Apostle
	lumbago	Lawrence
M	mental illness	Benedict Joseph Labre; Bibiana; Christina the Astonishing; Drogo; Dymphna; Fillan; Giles; Job; Margaret of Cortona; Maria Fortunata Viti; Medard; Michelina; Osmund; Raphaela
	migraine	Gereon; Severus of Avranches; Ulbadus Baldassini
	milk, loss of by nursing women	Margaret of Antioch
	miscarriage, against	Catherine of Sienna; Catherine of Sweden; Eulalia
	miscarriage prevention	Catherine of Sweden
	muteness	Drogo
N	near sightedness, short sightedness	Clarus, Abbot
	nerve or neurological disease, against	Bartholomew the Apostle; Dymphna
	nursing mothers	Concordia; Martina

O	obsession	Quirinus
P	pain relief	Madron
	pandemic	Edmund the Martyr
	paralysis	Catald; Osmund; Wolfgang
	physical spouse abuse, against; victims of spouse abuse, against	Rita of Cascia
	plague, against	Adrian of Nicomedia; Catald; Cuthbert; Erhard of Regensburg; Francis of Paola; Francis Xavier; George; Genevieve; Gregory the Great; Macarius of Antioch; Roch (Rocco); Sebastian; Valentine; Walburga
	poison sufferers	Benedict, Abbot; John the Apostle; Pirmin
	pregnant women, pregnancy	Anne; Anthony of Padua; Elizabeth; Gerard Majella; Joseph; Margaret (or Marina) of Antioch; Raymond Nonnatus; Ulric
R	rape victims	Agatha; Agnes of Rome; Antona Messina; Dymphna; Joan of Arc; Maria Goretti; Pierina Morosini; Potamiaena; Solange; Zita
	rheumatism, arthritis	Alphonus Maria de Liguori; Coloman; James the Greater; Killian; Servatus
	respiratory problems	Bernadine of Sienna
	ruptures, against Osmund	Drogo; Florentius of Strasburg;
S	scrofulous diseases	Balbina; Marculf; Mark the Evangelist
	skin disease	Anthony the Abbot; George; Marculf; Peregrine Laziosi; Roch (Rocco)
	skin rashes	Anthony the Abbot; George; Marculf; Peregrine Laziosi; Roch (Rocco)
	sleepwalkers, sleepwalking	Dymphna
	smallpox	Matthias
	snakebite victims	Hilary; Paul

	spasms	John the Baptist
	sterility, against	Agatha; Anne; Anthony of Padua; Casilda of Toledo; Felicity; Fiacre; Francis of Paola; Giles; Henry II; Margaret of Antioch; Medard; Philomena; Rita of Cascia; Theobald Roggeri
	stillborn children	Edmund
	stomach disease, stomach trouble	Brice; Charles Borromeo; Erasmus; Timothy; Wolfgang
	stroke	Andrew Avellino; Wolfgang
	struma	Balbina; Marculf; Mark the Evangelist
	surgery patients	Infant of Prague
	syphilis	Fiacre; George; Symphoroian of Autun
T	throat diseases, against	Andrew the Apostle; Blaise; Etheldreda; Godelieve; Ignatius of Antioch; Lucy of Syracuse; Swithbert
	toothaches	Apollonia; Christopher; Elizabeth of Hungary; Ida of Nivelles; Kea; Medard
	tuberculosis	Pantaleon; Thérèse of Lisieux
	twitching, against	Bartholomew the Apostle; Cornelius
	typhus, against	Adelard
U	ulcers, against	Charles Borromeo; Job
V	venereal disease	Fiacre
	verbal spousal abuse	Anne Marie Taigi; Godelieve; Monica
	vertigo, against	Ulric
W	whooping cough, against	Blaise; Winoc
	women in labor	Anne; Erasmus; John of Bridlington; Margaret (or Marina) of Antioch; Margaret of Fontana; Mary of Oignies
	women who wish to be mothers	Andrew the Apostle
	wounds	Aldegundis; Marciana; Rita of Cascia

Prayer Intentions

Use the space below to record the names of those you visit. Keep them in your personal prayers. Oftentimes, those you visit will ask you to pray for particular intentions. You can use this space to write down these intentions for continued prayer.

Prayer Intentions

Use the space below to record the names of those you visit. Keep them in your personal prayers. Oftentimes, those you visit will ask you to pray for particular intentions. You can use this space to write down these intentions for continued prayer.

Prayer Intentions

Use the space below to record the names of those you visit. Keep them in your personal prayers. Oftentimes, those you visit will ask you to pray for particular intentions. You can use this space to write down these intentions for continued prayer.

Prayer Intentions

Use the space below to record the names of those you visit. Keep them in your personal prayers. Oftentimes, those you visit will ask you to pray for particular intentions. You can use this space to write down these intentions for continued prayer.